What Submissives Want to Know

Kate Kinsey

DEDICATION

To Sir. Always.

CONTENTS

INTRODUCTION

Is there such a thing as a stupid question?

One of the reasons I wrote my first non-fiction book, *How to be a Healthy and Happy Submissive*, was because people asked me the same questions over and over. It wasn't that I didn't want to answer; for efficiency, it just made sense to write out my best, most complete answer, and then it was there for everybody who wanted to know.

I'll let you in on a secret: writing this stuff doesn't pay my bills. It barely pays my tab at Starbucks. Good thing I don't do it for the money! My point is that I have a full-time job, and when you factor in writing books under two names (vanilla and kinky), plus trying to have a life where I do important things like laundry, rubbing the cat's tummy or maybe even getting tied up once in a while, there just aren't enough hours in a day for me to give every question in my inbox the attention it deserves.

Hence, another book to fill the gaps. But one of the things I've found is that just as there are no stupid questions, neither are there any new questions. Not really.

So, you've picked up this book because you have at least one question burning in your mind, and here I am telling you it's nothing new. This doesn't mean your question isn't valid, or important. On the contrary, a question that has been asked before means it's truly wisdom worth seeking, because so many others before you have needed the answer. It doesn't mean that your question isn't deeply and intensely personal, because every question comes wrapped in its own emotions and circumstances.

Obviously, the one most often asked is "How do I find a dominant?" or "How do I get started in BDSM?" No matter how many times that question is asked, it remains crucially important. At some point, all of us have asked that question. (For the answer to that one, you should consult *How to be a Healthy and Happy Submissive*. It takes a whole book to answer that one.)

But at their core, most of the letters that fill my inbox daily tend to fall into certain categories. When you look at them closely, you see that questions that appear to be completely different actually have the same question underneath.

One submissive wrote to me that she was concerned that a potential dominant wanted her to find a playmate for him; another wondered if it was "normal" for a dominant to punish her by refusing to talk to her. These are actually the same question: "How is a good dominant supposed to act?"

So that's why I put this book out into the world: because if someone else has asked these questions, then it's highly likely that someone else out there is wondering the same things. Even if you haven't ever lost sleep over whether or not you are too alpha to be a good submissive, there is probably something in the question or the answer that will have meaning for you, even if the ultimate answer to that question is simply: you can be anything you want to be.

These are real letters and answers that have come through my website or Fetlife.com. Names and certain identifying details have been changed, naturally, and the authors have given their permission for me to use their questions in this book. In a couple of instances I have expanded my answer or edited the original question for brevity.

I'm going to assume that you've already read *How to be a Healthy and Happy Submissive*, or some other book that lays a good foundation for understanding how BDSM relationships work. I can't stress enough that knowledge is power. The more you know, the less likely it is that anyone can take advantage of you.

Let me go a step further: if you're not willing to study up on this stuff, then you shouldn't be messing around with such a powerful magic that can literally put your life in someone else's hands. You don't have to read my book—or even finish this one – but for God's sake, read something!

Some things I want to make clear here:

- I don't claim to have all the answers. I am not a professional counselor. I simply share my experience and what I've learned throughout the past fifteen years as honestly as possible. The most important thing I've ever learned is this:

everybody has an opinion, and no one has the only, ultimate answer. Read this, and if it makes sense to you, then use it. Take what you need and leave the rest. Don't ever let anybody else tell you they know the "right" way to do this. There is no right way, as long as you are safe, sane and consensual. Right is what works for you and your partner.

- These questions are asked by someone *from their point of view*. For all I know, the writer has either deliberately or unconsciously left out some important detail. Often, the person on the other side of the question (i.e. the "mean dominant") has reasons of their own, and we don't get to hear them. Let's face it, there are individuals out there who live in their own little bubbles of reality; you've probably met a few and have learned the hard way to take everything they say with a grain of salt.

- Most situations are never as clear as they may appear in these questions. Most often, I try to point out things they should consider in order to find the answer for themselves. The person asking is the one who ultimately has to decide, because they are the ones who are going to have to live with the decision.

A friend who did a read-through of this book said that perhaps I was doing a disservice to my readers by "harping" on *their* rights, and *their* needs.

"You sound like you're telling them to become feminists," he said, "not submissives."

"*Someone* needs to make sure they understand that they do have rights," I said, more than a little peeved.

Perhaps it does seem a contradiction to advise submissives to be assertive, but it's really not. Submissives need to be confident and assertive even more so than "vanilla" women because they are putting so much more trust in their partners. A vanilla woman doesn't routinely trust her partner to tie her up and do potentially harmful things to her.

You should only be a good submissive if you have a good dominant. The trouble is learning to tell the difference between a good dominant and a bad one.

So let's go see what's in the mailbag, shall we?

1 HOW DO I DEAL WITH MY DOMINANT'S DISPLEASURE?

Hello Kate,

I'm just starting a D/s relationship and we are both brand new at the D/s lifestyle, and we are mostly doing this through email exchanges thus far.

Is it normal as his sub to feel extremely sensitive to my Dom's corrections? Am I taking this too seriously? I don't know if I'm being too sensitive. I want to please him so much, and his instructions have sometimes been ambiguous, so we've had a few miscommunications. When he states displeasure, it's pulling my heartstrings. When a Dom says he displeased, are they really upset with you, or is it part of the play?

—Kelly

Kelly:

What you're describing isn't unusual. Submissives are by nature eager to please, so they are especially sensitive to correction from their dominant. Often, we don't even need to hear them say anything. When I see disappointment on my Sir's face, I just want to crawl in a hole.

You ask: is he really upset, or is it part of the play? It depends on the context. For example, if you're doing a school girl scene, and he frowns at you and says, "That skirt is entirely too short, Miss Thing. You need a spanking" -- that's part of the scene.

If he told you to wear no panties, and you're wearing panties, then he is probably upset with a valid reason. You didn't do as you were told.

I've known of some dominants who will do things simply to keep their submissive off balance, and that's a practice that frankly pisses me off. They do it as part of that whole "breaking 'em down to build 'em up" mentality, and because keeping the sub in a constant state of anxiety feeds their ego and sense of control. I'm sure some dominant out there has written a book where they explain in detail why this is an important tool. But I believe that a D/s relationship can't work if both aren't being honest at all times. How can you put all your life in the hands of a dominant if you can't trust him to tell you the truth about what he's feeling?

Some dominants use that "play disappointment" as a part of

humiliation play and/or emotional sadism, which works for some people, but not all. Pretending to be angry or disappointed with a submissive that has genuinely tried his/her best is a terrible breach of trust, and to do it repeatedly, in my opinion, is a form of emotional abuse.

But you mention miscommunication, and that seems to me to be the heart of the matter, because communication is the single most important thing in a D/s relationship. You can't be safe, you can't be honest, and you can't be trusting, if you can't communicate. No amount of skill with ropes or floggers is worth a hill of beans if you can't communicate.

You can learn a lot by how each of you reacts to miscommunication. Are you respectful when you tell him that you felt his instructions were unclear, or do you whine or accuse? Does he listen when you try to give him honest, respectful feedback, or does he get defensive and impatient?

Both of you need to carefully consider the situation whenever there is a miscommunication or lack of clarity. Dominants need to learn how to be better dominants, just as we submissives always strive to improve in obedience and devotion. If he seems consistently unwilling to listen, or to ever take responsibility for miscommunication, you might want to rethink whether he's the dominant for you.

If he has a valid reason for being displeased, and tells you so, then your job is to listen. In your own mind and heart, think carefully about what has displeased him. Make sure that you have set aside your ego, your hurt feelings, and your desire to be right. Those are things a submissive needs to let go of if she wants to serve to the best of her abilities.

You mustn't ever be afraid or reluctant to speak up when you feel he's been unfair, but you must be sure you're being honest with yourself, and do it respectfully. When you are in the wrong, you must suck it up, feel the hurt but don't let it turn you into a useless puddle on the floor. Put that energy instead to making amends and figuring out how you can avoid repeating the behavior that displeased him.

If he's new to this, then you both need to admit that you're going to have to take it slowly. It's hard for a new dominant to get a feel for just how dominant he needs or wants to be. He can be any way he wants to be, as long as it works for you both. Some tend to overdo it in the beginning, for fear of someone finding out that they are unsure of themselves.

This is why I wish there were more mentors and books for dominants, because they need as much, if not more, guidance in the beginning as submissives. An important component of a good dominant is confidence, and that comes with experience. In the meantime, a dominant needs to understand that he/she is not expected to be perfect, that is all right for them to ask for feedback from their submissives, and for them to admit when they have made a mistake and to correct it.

Often, people assume that being the dominant means they call all the shots and the submissive just jumps when he hollers "Frog!" But a good dominant carries an enormous responsibility to mentor, to train, to motivate, and to care for his/her submissive or slave. A good dominant is supposed to help you grow and become not just a better submissive, but a better person.

His impatience may come in part from his own uncertainty about how to do this. When you question for more details, it forces him to realize that he either didn't communicate things well or think through all the ramifications of his instructions; hence he feels like he's been caught short and that embarrasses him. Or he could feel that you are questioning his authority, rather than his instructions.

I understand exactly what you mean about being detail-oriented. Everybody wants their subordinate to get things done, but until those subordinates learn exactly what is expected of them, and how much leeway the boss allows them in making minor decisions on their own, the detail-oriented subordinate or submissive can test their patience. That's where the boss needs to remember that he/she is teaching you how to please them, and to be patient.

Take an extra moment before asking him more questions, and see if you can make a reasonable deduction. I've learned to do this myself just recently. Sometimes in my eagerness, I start asking questions, and then realize I already have the information; I just got ahead of myself.

Again, you two need to discuss this. You need to make sure he understands your questions come out of the desire to please him, not to question his authority. It is perfectly acceptable to ask him for additional positive feedback.

2 HOW DO I TELL MY VANILLA PARTNER I'M KINKY?

Dear Kate:

I have been looking into being a submissive for a while now, almost a year. I don't know if you could call me a newbie sub or not because I haven't had a real sub-dom relationship. I'm with my boyfriend of two years now. I have hinted to him multiple times about wanting him to take more control. He likes very much when I do what he says. I know he would like the idea of it. I'm into calling my dom "daddy," (which I don't believe he would be interested in), as well as being tied down and blindfolded, etc., (which I do believe he would like too).

I don't know how to tell him what I want with out coming off as "too kinky" or him finding it awkward. I just don't know how to tell him about what I want. I'm kinda into the age play part of it, but I don't know, and that's my point. I want HIM to be the one to explore these things with me. I've always wanted to meet a real dom who knows what he's doing, but I love my current boyfriend so much and don't want to lose him or anything like that, I just don't know what to do. Help??

— *Brittany*

Brittany:

You are in a very common situation: how do I tell someone I love I'm kinky?

I don't have a magic answer for you, but as much as I hate the whole *Fifty Shades of Grey* phenomenon, it has a least given people a very accessible conversation starter. So many people have read it just out of curiosity, because everyone was talking about it. Which makes it easy for you to say, "These women at work were talking about this movie; wanna watch it with me?" Which is an excellent opportunity to see his reactions, and to tell him, "Gosh, that spanking scene made me hot…"

Movies and books are a very good way to start talking about your fantasies. If not *Fifty Shades*, (I loathed the books for all kinds of reasons, and have not seen the movie because I didn't want to put another dime in E.L. James' overflowing purse), then try *Secretary* (one of my favorite movies of any kind), or even the rather silly *Exit to Eden*. The key is not to just talk about your fantasies, but to find out what *his* are.

You can also approach it playfully by suggesting role-play. Confess that as a kid you loved playing cowboys and Indians, and liked it when you got tied up!

Most men like to think of themselves as a sexual adventurer, so appeal to his open-mindedness, and praise him for any way he might have introduced you to new things in the past. Then tell him that what you are suggesting is a way not just to increase your pleasure, but to increase the intimacy between you. You want to explore this with *him*.

I can almost guarantee you that if you share just one little bitty part of your fantasies, he will come up with something he's always wanted to try. He's probably far more afraid of you being turned off by him suggesting something "freaky." Let's face it, men are almost expected to be "perverts" while they assume most "nice" women are not nearly as interested in sex as they are. Of course, with porn these days going further and further into every taboo imaginable and inventing new ones everyday, that's changing for a lot of younger men. As recently as the early 80s, many men hesitated to ask for anal sex; now, younger men almost expect it*, and some teens don't consider it "having sex" at all.

But before you ever bring it up with him, make sure that you are comfortable with your own kink. The more relaxed and confident you sound when you bring it up, the more natural it sounds to him. Do some reading so you can tell him why what you're asking for is something a lot of people enjoy, and that it's not any kind of mental illness. I suggest *Screw the Roses, Send Me the Thorns* as a good place to start your education. It's written with a light tone and some humor, and it's good to have it around *after* you talk to him so he can read it as well. (Or you can read it to him. Naked. In bed.)

Just talk to him. Take it a little at a time, see what kind of response you get, and then take it a little further. Don't show up with a leather harness, a whip and a coil of rope all at once; start slowly. Perhaps just a pair of leather cuffs, or a single silk scarf as a blindfold.

(One warning about bondage: don't jump in too deep, too fast. Bondage is one of the most common ways accidents can happen in BDSM. There is good information online and on Amazon.)

As for the daddy part: hold off on that a bit. Do some reading about "littles" and "age play" and "daddy doms" to make sure you can explain what it's about, in all its variations. Most people think it's about incest, and that is most often not the case. It's about a kind of loving, nurturing, protective relationship modeled on a father/daughter relationship. Many of the daddy/baby girl relationships don't include sex at all. It is an often misunderstood kink.

If you don't belong to FetLife.com, sign up. You can find a lot of information there on every possible topic. Don't rely on porn!

As to what younger "vanilla" people expect sexually these days, I'm not the best judge. For one thing, I'm in my fifties. For another, I move in a pretty kinky community of friends, where talking about everything from whippings to blowjobs is as natural as discussing who won Sunday's game. I sometimes forget that not everybody talks about deep throat techniques over brunch.

3 SHOULD A DOMINANT ASK ME TO FIND SEX PARTNERS FOR HIM?

Dear Kate:

I am a newbie. I have met someone who tells me he has been a dominant all his life. He says that we will have a contract, safe words, and will be exclusive to each other. He says that we will have open communication and full disclosure.

I have been given several tasks to prove myself worthy. I have read about this before. Is it really a common thing? Also he wants me to find him a "pet" to service his needs when I cannot. He says he will find me one as well, and neither of us are to play with our pets without the other giving full authority to do so. When I have completed this task, then I "will be worthy to kneel before him."

The tasks that I have been given so far are to obtain the pet, and service him in a "risky" sneaky way.

I am now working on a way to meet with him and to go about it secretly. He seems to like that. I have found this difficult.

13

I asked him to talk about negotiations and he didn't want to discuss it. What do you think? Is this an unusual task to be given before our negotiations are completed?

- Charlotte

Dear Charlotte:

This guy seems to know enough to say the right things: a contract, open communication, etc. But so far it doesn't sound like you're seeing proof of any of that. Always pay attention to what a dominant *does,* not just what he *says.*

I've found that many dominants will try to get away with whatever they can. That includes the "Bring-Me-Some-Strange-Pussy" assignment.

It's not unusual that one would give you tasks, and whether it is a good or bad thing depends entirely on what kind of tasks he's assigning. Write an essay on what kind of relationship you are looking for? That's good!

Find someone to "service" him? In my opinion, that's just plain cheesy. Unless, of course, it turns you on in some way to pimp for him. I've known some subs, usually those into humiliation, who are turned on by being forced to watch the dominant have sex with someone else.

While some dominants DO ask a sub or slave to find "pets" or "fuck toys" for them, it is generally bad manners to do it before you are even in a proper relationship. Aside from the obvious perk of getting someone else to play with, some do it before the deal is done because they want to be absolutely clear that they are not going to be monogamous, and that jealousy will not be tolerated. In some ways, that's a good thing for the submissive to find out in the early stages, rather than months down the road.

Which is one of the biggest red flags here: he promised you an exclusive relationship, but he's already asking you to bring in other women? Liar, liar, pants on fire.

How do YOU feel about being asked to do something like this? If you are uncomfortable with this at all — and I suspect you are or you wouldn't have asked — then tell this man so. How he reacts will tell you a lot. Don't let anybody push you into things you don't feel good about it.

What did you mean about being asked to meet him in "risky, sneaky ways"? "Risky" and "sneaky" can mean a lot of things. Does he mean sneaking off to give him a blowjob in his car on your lunch hour? Okay, that can be fun and exciting. But does he mean seeing him in private without telling anybody where you are going? BUZZZ! Not a good idea! Cheating on your partner or his? BUZZZ! Not a good idea! Doing something that could get you arrested? Terrible, terrible idea!

But the two biggest problems I see here are: 1) he doesn't want to discuss negotiations, even though he promised you that he would; and 2) he wants you to prove yourself worthy.

First, walk away from anyone who won't negotiate with you. That's a huge red flag. You have every right to know exactly what you're being asked to submit to, as well as every right to state limits and needs of your own.

Second, why are *you* the only one having to prove your worthiness? One of the hardest concepts to get through our submissive skulls is that being submissive doesn't mean we simply accept what we are given. We are so attuned to, and turned on by, the idea of being the supplicant, on our knees, offering obedience and devotion, that often we don't even notice that someone is being a total ass. We forget that we have power, even after we submit ourselves to someone else's.

Do you need to prove yourself worthy? I guess you could put it that way. That's part of negotiating every relationship, vanilla or kinky. But it's a two-way street.

He has to prove himself worthy of your submission as well. It's actually far more important that he measure up to your standards, because he is the one that can endanger your physical, emotional and mental health. You are the one who is willing to give your power over to his keeping.

Many submissives are so deliriously excited in that first flush of infatuation that we overlook a lot of a dominant's shortcomings. In the short run, maybe it doesn't matter so much that he's not open to negotiation, or good at communication – or so you think.

We all believe that once we've earned a dominant's love or ownership, he'll change. (Sound familiar, married ladies?) Take my word for it: he won't. If he's not offering good, honest communication now, it's because he doesn't care. He's not in this for the long haul. You're a plaything to be enjoyed for the moment.

And that's not always a bad thing – enjoying the moment, that is. Casual play can be wonderful and exciting. Submission during play doesn't have to be rooted in a romantic relationship that you want to last forever, just as sexual flings don't have to be a prelude to a lifelong partnership. But be sure you know what it is that you want. Submissives lose their hearts so easily.

4 IS THERE SUCH AN ANIMAL AS A MONOGAMOUS DOMINANT?

Dear Kate:

I've always been submissive all my life in one way or another, but never on my terms. I want this now for myself.

I am a loving and caring woman with a big heart. I want to find love, not just someone to use me as a sex toy or as part of his harem. It is just a fantasy to think I might find a dominant looking for his soul mate, just as I am? Is it possible to have love, sex and submission all at the same time?

- Donna

Dear Donna:

Yes, you can find a dominant that is looking for his soul mate and is monogamous, but it won't be easy. Then again, finding a soul mate in the vanilla realm is no walk in the park either.

Unfortunately, you do limit the pool of potential partners when you add in "dominant" and "monogamous" to your shopping list. They are out there, it's just going to take time, patience and work to find them.

Does that mean you shouldn't try? Hell, no! If you don't ask for what you want, nobody's gonna just drop it in your lap. I know lots of happily monogamous kinksters. I also know a lot of happily polyamorous kinksters.

It's true that many dominants are either polyamorous or practice open relationships. Part of the reason for this is simply that people who have questioned one societal norm in favor of BDSM find it easier to question other conventional ideas like monogamy. That's why you find so many kinksters who are either poly or into open relationships, as well as pagan. We are people that looked around at what everyone else was doing and decided it wasn't right for us. We opened our minds to other options. Once you've found that inner courage to break with traditional norms, everything is up for grabs.

But there are still plenty of monogamous kinksters. It's a little hard to tell sometimes, because many who are completely happy with keeping their D/s relationship at home behind closed doors with their committed partner simply aren't as visible. When you venture out into the "public" BDSM/kink community, you're more likely to see those either seeking a new partner or multiple partners.

It's no different than going out to a vanilla bar looking to meet someone special: the happy, monogamous couples are at home or having dinner with friends, and many of the monogamous singles have grown tired of the social scene.

Let's face it: harems are a dominant fantasy. Many just want multiple partners. Many are open to their submissives having other partners, too.

Finding a monogamous dominant takes patience and a firm refusal to settle for less than you really want. Finding a special someone – either kinky or vanilla – is hard, so you should be prepared for this to take a while.

Look in the obvious places for a dominant: FetLife being my personal best advice, and your local kink community, through munches and parties and other social or educational events. But don't forget to look in other places as well.

There are kinky folks all over. I've run into many at work, at college reunions, on Facebook, in book clubs, and even at the local Kinko's when I was having some promotional materials for my local club printed. Those are just the ones that revealed themselves. Who knows how many more I say hello to every day?

Another good reason to looking in non-kinky places is that you are more than just your kink. If you are looking for a long-term relationship, you want to find someone with whom you share more than just BDSM. I constantly have to remind newbies creating their first online profile to include something more than just a list of their sexual desires. What are you interested in besides good sex and bondage? Do you have a hobby? What kinds of books and movies and music do you like? Tell the world something about what makes you who you are, and what you want not just from a dominant, but from life.

Having a profile that paints a portrait of a real, flesh-and-blood human being increases the chances that another such person will find you.

5 WHAT IF I'M NOT A SKINNY MINNIE?

Dear Kate:

I want to explore BDSM, but I'm self-conscious about my body. I'm a bigger girl. Wide hips, big bum, large breasts, thick thighs. And people have always called me fat for that reason, so I'm scared. Scared of how people would see me.

- Curvy

Dear Curvy:

I understand body image issues. As an adult, I've worn everything from a size six to a size twenty-four and back -- twice.

You are not the only one to feel this way. Even skinny girls hate the way they look. Every woman I know thinks she's too fat or too thin, or her breasts are too small or her butt is too big, or her nose is too pointy or her teeth are too crooked. None of us ever thinks we're fine just the way we are without working hard to accept ourselves.

Much about how we feel about ourselves has been programmed into us by the media. You are a real person. You are not an airbrushed photograph. The only "perfect" is being perfectly comfortable with yourself no matter what your size or height or eye color or shoe size.

People in the kink community are actually very accepting of different body types. I've played in the local dungeon with a lot of naked women and very few of them were anywhere near "model" proportions, including me. When I walked into a dungeon for the first time, I wanted to play badly enough that I said to hell with feeling too fat. I realized that if I waited until I was thin and beautiful, I was never going to be ready, and I'd already waited half of my life.

(An interesting aside here: you almost never see a naked dominant in the dungeon. Someone once told me it's because it's hard to maintain your authority when people see you in all your natural glory.)

I'm not going to bore you with all the "beauty is only skin deep, it's what you are on the inside that matters" crap. I call it crap because everybody says that all the time, and while it's true, it doesn't change the way the world works.

Pretty people get treated better. But that leads to this old lady of fifty telling you that you are still very, very young. You've got a lot of time ahead of you, and it will fly by faster than you can possibly imagine. MAKE THE MOST OF IT. If the way you feel about your size is going to hold you back from living the life you want, then by God, change it!

How you feel about yourself matters more than how big you are. You can learn to accept yourself as you are, or you can decide to change it. You need to do one or the other, or you're going to let the way you feel about how you look limit what you do with your life.

More important than how you look is your health. I've got a lot of health problems that came up in my forties because of the extra weight I've carried most of my life. Severe arthritis in knees and ankles, and I've started saving for that first knee replacement in my future. I also have adult onset diabetes. If I could go back and kick my 35 year-old ass and say, "Get healthy now," I would. (Of course, would I listen?) It only gets harder with age. There are things I still want to do in my life but my weight is holding me back because of health issues.

If you want to do serious bondage, lose the weight and take up yoga immediately. Many types of play require flexibility, strength and endurance.

Think about what you want out of your life, and then do everything within your power to be ready to grab every opportunity that comes your way.

6 WHAT IF I LOSE MY DOMINANT?

Dear Kate:

I've been in a D/s relationship for two years now, and at first it was amazing. But in the last couple of months, things have not been going so well. Now, he says he is "releasing" me and has moved out.

I've been through break-ups before, but this is killing me. I honestly don't know how to keep going. I just want to curl up and die.

Do you have any advice? Being his submissive was such a central part of my life, what do I do now?

- Heartbroken

Dear Heartbroken:

My heart goes out to you. Submissives tend to fall in love with dominants hard and fast. When a D/s relationship breaks up, it's even worse than any vanilla breakup you've ever experienced.

Why? Several reasons. First, you've been intimate with this person in ways you may never have been with anyone else. You've shared your deepest, darkest secrets. You've done things for this person you never thought you'd ever do for anyone, and done it with gratitude for being allowed the privilege.

For most submissives, all of our relationships have been colored by our submissive desires even before we knew what to call it. We are prone to deep attachments, and many of us learn early on to keep a tight hold on our emotions. We try to hold back, because we've been hurt so many times before, or had lovers turn away from us because we were too needy, too clingy, too intense, just *too much*.

Then we discover this thing called BDSM, and suddenly it all makes sense. There's nothing wrong with us. We're not too needy, too clingy, too intense. We are, instead, special creatures with an enormous capacity for devotion that takes another special person to recognize and appreciate.

So we take the plunge. We jump off the cliff and soar into a joyful satisfaction and pleasure that we always dreamed of. We open ourselves up to another person, with no holding back, no pretense, no attempt at self-preservation. We sacrifice ego for obedience; we build our world around the person who makes all our fantasies come true.

And then it all goes wrong. It doesn't matter why. The

relationship ends, and we are absolutely devastated. We took off all our armor, and now we're left with nothing to protect us from the heartbreak.

- **Allow yourself time to grieve.** Accept that it's just going to suck for a while, but it will get better. Be prepared to experience some or all of the stages of grief: denial, anger, guilt, acceptance and adaptation. This is something everyone has to go through. If anyone tells you to get over it, tell them to go fuck themselves.

- **Hold tight to the knowledge that this is not the last love you will ever find.** I know, it's the kind of thing people say and you want to punch them in the face. But it's true.

- **Take care of yourself.** That means eat reasonably, and get plenty of rest. Get some exercise to help endorphins kick in, and don't rely on drugs or alcohol to numb the pain.

- **Consider play with friends.** You don't want to go rushing into another relationship, but if you have a friend or two with whom you are comfortable playing with casually, consider making a play date or getting together at a party. Sometimes a good flogging or some other non-sexual play can have a very therapeutic or cathartic effect, and get those endorphins flowing. This doesn't work for everyone, but it's something to think about. (At one of my lowest points after a break-up, I asked a female dominant at a party to cane me, because I hated canes and all I really wanted was to sob my heart out. This comes in very handy if you have to be out in public and can't stop sniveling.)

- **Talk to someone.** Talk to friends, or if you really think you may harm yourself, find a counselor. The National Coalition for Sexual Freedom has a list of kink-aware professionals that includes therapists all over the country that understand the dynamics of your relationship. Find the list at the following link on their website: https://ncsfreedom.org/resources/kink-aware-professionals-directory/kap-directory-homepage.html

- **Pamper yourself.** Make yourself do at least one thing every day that you enjoy, whether that is listening to a favorite CD, taking a bubble bath, or watching funny cat videos online. (*General Hospital* and strawberry ice cream kept me from self-harm at one point.)

- **Do not rush into another relationship.** You need to get your feet back under you before getting back on the horse. If you rush it, you risk making bad decisions. YOU HAVE TIME. USE IT.

- **Write it out.** Get it all out in a journal or a blog or whatever. It really does help to process the emotions and consider what happened, what mistakes you may have made and what you learned from the experience. If you are in a situation where you would normally post to your blog or FetLife page, but feel you can't now without embarrassing yourself or someone you love, you can set up a "sock puppet" account under a new anonymous name; it allows you to put your pain out there honestly without embarrassment to you or anyone else, and without fueling the local gossip factory. (Yes, I have a sock puppet for expressing deep pain, screaming frustration and ranting tempter tantrums. It helps to draw the poison out when I need to vent without the personal fallout.)

- **Use your support network**. If you belong to FetLife, you can find wonderful support among people who've been through the same things. From time to time, in the rough spots, I've relied on the kindness of strangers, and it made all the difference. See "sock puppet" above.

- You're allowed to **take time away from kink** if it helps you heal. The kinky world will still be there when you're ready to go back.

- Mostly, just keep breathing. It will get better.

7 CAN I BUILD MY OWN DOMINANT?

Dear Kate:

I got into BDSM erotica a couple years ago and kept feeling that there's something missing in my relationships because they're so vanilla.

I'm semi-serious with someone now, and as hard as he tries to do the stuff I like, I'm not truly satisfied. I crave someone with more experience who enjoys it too because they like being dominant, instead of me always being the teacher. Do you think I'll ever be able to turn my boyfriend into the dominant I want without ruining our relationship? Or do you have any advice?

- Kimberly

Dear Kimberly:

Your question hits home for me, because I have been exactly where you are, and I know how frustrating it can be. For most of my life, I attempted to turn boyfriends into dominants. It was always obvious their hearts weren't in it, and one was so uncomfortable with the whole idea, it ended the relationship entirely. For a submissive that wants to please and serve, it's awkward as hell when you feel someone else is doing something only to please you.

Can you turn your boyfriend into your dominant? Generally speaking, dominance is not something you can teach someone. Then again, some men have it in them, they have simply repressed it all their lives because society has told them to hide all that "macho" crap, and always be respectful to women. How can a man spank you when he was told all his life not to hit a girl?

It can take time for a man to get his head around the fact that he can respect a woman and still be the one in control, while walking that fine line between being dominant and being a bullying asshole. It's a matter of having the consent of the woman in question, and building a relationship on things they both want and need. Some men need you to give them permission to even turn their minds in that direction, and some will never be able to get past it.

Have you just told him, "I'd like for you to tie me up?" or have you really discussed in detail what BDSM is, how dominance and submission works, and why it turns you on? Perhaps if you both read something like *Screw the Roses, Send Me the Thorns* together, he'd get a better understanding of what you're after. It might also loosen him up to see that other people do this all the time.

Consider how much time you have invested in this current relationship, and what it's worth to you. The kink isn't everything, but I know from experience — and from the experience of others — that longing for BDSM can remain an itch you can't quite scratch for a long, long time. Sooner or later, you either do something about it, or you regret it. Sometimes you do the wrong thing about it (i.e. cheat on the one you love) and you regret that, too.

Is it possible that he would be willing to let you explore the local kinky community? It's possible you can find a dominant that would be willing to work with you both, and show him more of the psychological aspects that go along with the physical.

It's risky and there's a chance that it will damage or end the relationship, but it might be worth a try. A lot depends on his willingness, your patience and the integrity of a cooperative dominant. A female dominant might be an option your partner would be more comfortable with.

The important thing is to talk about it, and see where you might be able to find common ground from which to start.

8 CAN A SUBMISSIVE BECOME A DOMINANT?

Dear Kate:

I have been dating a guy who's into BDSM. I've been into kinky sex before but without the specific roles of dom/sub. However, in his past relationship, he was the submissive. We agreed that he'd be the dominant as I don't have much experience in this area but I'm pretty nervous as we're both going to be trying stuff we've not done before. Can a submissive become a dominant? Do you have any advice?

- Lisa

Dear Lisa:

First, kudos for being open to trying new things!

The best advice is always: read up. The issue of roles — and whether or not someone can be both, or switch roles when they chose to — is a complicated matter that some debate endlessly.

There are several schools of thought on dominant/submissive roles:

1) You are born dominant or submissive:

Some (mostly dominants) will insist that you are born either one or the other. That may be true for some people, and if they believe that about themselves, who am I or anyone else to disagree?

But I don't believe anyone should make such sweeping judgments about other people; they can't know what feelings, desires, and urges exist deep in another person's psyche, or how life experiences may have shaped them.

This theory gets really annoying if you come across someone who insists that women are "born" submissive and men are "born" dominant. That's just plain bullshit.

2) The sliding scale of dominance/submission:

Another theory — and the one that I personally subscribe to — is that we all exist on a sliding scale of dominance/submission. We all have a bit of both in us, and we respond differently to other people who may be more one or the other than ourselves.

Example: I am a submissive in the kink world. It is what I enjoy and what (most of the time) I am most comfortable with, and certainly what arouses me. Yet there are many dominants that I feel are actually less dominant than I am. My mind and body simply do not respond to them. I couldn't possibly submit to them. For another submissive, they may be perfect.

3) It's your choice:

Life forces us to slip in and out of roles all the time, so we can assume the role of dominant or submissive in a situation as we choose. Consider that no matter how dominant a person is, they have to submit to teachers, employers, and law enforcement if they don't want to end up ignorant, unemployed or in jail. Likewise, if a person can't be dominant with their children, students, employees, etc., life is going to roll them flatter than an armadillo on an Alabama highway.

If I see a situation in which no one is willing to take the lead, but things need to get done, I step easily into a more dominant role. There are few things as frustrating as trying to get a group of submissives to decide where to go for dinner. In those situations, I'm always the one to say, "Damn it, I'm starving; we're going to Olive Garden."

(Many people assume I am a dominant. I was explaining *Fifty Shades* to a vanilla friend, and she said, "So, you're Mr. Grey." I laughed and asked why she would think I was the dominant. She looked at me like I was crazy and said, "Because you just *are*.")

Some people will actually choose the role in kink that is

completely opposite to what they are in real life. The high-powered executive, for example, who makes tough decisions and leads all day long, may find an enormous relief and sexual gratification in submitting to someone else in the bedroom or dungeon.

Some change roles depending on their partner. I've been dominant with other people a few times, but I could never dominate my Sir.

4) Bottoming/Topping:

Now, I've given you all this confusing information, and your situation might be something else entirely that is much more simple. Are you talking about "topping" rather than dominating?

Dominating someone means they surrender their power to you. They will gain their pleasure from pleasing you. It's more about the relationship dynamic, and usually (but not always) extends outside the bedroom.

Topping, on the other hand, is more about what you actually do. If someone likes to be tied up or spanked, that doesn't really mean they are submitting or submissive. It just means they like having those things done to them. I have known many dominants that liked to bottom, and have even trained their submissive to do those things to them as part of pleasing them.

If by saying he has "always been the submissive," he actually means he was the bottom in their activities, then you and he shouldn't have any trouble exploring both or either role. But in the course of that exploration, you may find you really aren't comfortable with things like being tied up or spanked. Or you may discover you really like those activities, but don't enjoy submitting to him in other ways outside the bedroom such as letting him choose how you dress, calling him "Sir," etc.) Likewise, he may find he doesn't enjoy being in charge at all.

It's important that you are both honest and respect each other's feelings. A rejection of the role is not a rejection of your boyfriend or him rejecting you; it just means you need to explore some other options to find what does work for both of you.

5) Your role/relationship is whatever you want it to be:
Ultimately, the only rule in any of this is that you are safe, sane and consensual. If you want to dominant him only on Monday, Wednesday and Sunday, and only while he wears a pink tutu and army boots, that's perfectly okay. If it makes you both happy, go for it. Don't let anybody tell you otherwise.

9 HOW MUCH SHOULD I SHARE IN MY ONLINE PROFILE?

Dear Kate:

I've taken your advice and made an account on FetLife, but I haven't put up a picture and I didn't use my real name because I'm scared someone I know will find me. I know this is silly because that would require them being on there too!

- Julie

Dear Julie:

It's natural to feel a little hesitant. Different people have different reasons for not wanting their sexual inclinations to become public knowledge.

Many people -- including myself -- use a *scene name,* or screen name, simply to have a little discretionary buffer. Others don't worry about being "outed" as kinky, and they put their real names, cities, photos, you name it. It's really up to you and how much you feel comfortable with. Personally, I would advise against using your real name, or at least not your full name. We all put way too much info about ourselves out there, and I don't just mean kinky stuff.

I have a submissive friend who had someone she'd been talking to online suddenly show up at her front door. She hadn't told him her address, but he had enough details about her to track her down. If you want to tell someone what you do for a living ("I'm an accountant"), okay; just don't tell them where you work, or for whom you work, for example, until you know someone much, much better.

You don't have to put your photo out there, and I usually advise against it — not a standard headshot, at least. If you look around online, you'll see that people get creative with photos. Some people are open enough to put their faces online; others have some reason like jobs or families that they don't want a recognizable photo out there.

My Sir, for example, is a teacher, therefore he can't have his photo out there. I can't be completely "out" for several reasons. It would compromise my Sir, and possibly my chances for advancement in my real job. Plus, I have two different writing careers (one kinky, the other one vanilla) and their audiences do NOT overlap. But probably the most important reason is there are members of my family who, though they are aware of my lifestyle and okay with it, would be very uncomfortable with *their* friends and coworkers knowing about it. I would not cause them pain for anything in the world.

Some people use avatars, memes, cartoons or some artwork that they feel expresses something about them. I use my book covers. Some use photos that don't show their faces – a nice shot of their new boots or sexy heels, for example; or the more explicit (yet faceless) body shots. Just remember that whatever photo or art you use will affect the kinds of responses and friend requests that you get.

In other words, if you post a photo of yourself holding a penis in each hand, expect to get some very explicit come-ons looking for a quick hookup. Not that there's anything wrong with either the photo or the hook-ups. Some kinksters are exhibitionists at heart, and some people want to indulge their sexual appetites in a casual way.

I'll go a step further for the newbie submissive: it's okay to say you're new to this lifestyle, but don't go overboard saying, "I've never done anything like this, I'm practically a virgin, and I really want someone to help me get started..."

There are people out there – some dominants, and some just posers – who are particularly drawn to the inexperienced. It may be a completely innocent; it is exciting to introduce a new submissive to a whole world of new experiences! But then there are also those who seek the newbie because they are looking for someone unsure of herself, vulnerable and – perhaps most importantly – without an established support network of other more experienced kinksters. They think your lack of knowledge will keep you from seeing how inexperienced they are, or how much they are skirting the edges of safe, sane and consensual. They like that you don't have a support group, so you'll have no one to ask about things that are making you uncomfortable or to turn to if something bad happens. Watch out for those guys.

I've said this before elsewhere: spend some time and thought on crafting your profile. Don't just list your sexual preferences. Say something about who you are, the kind of relationship you hope to find, the values that are important to you. If there are things you absolutely are not interested in – perhaps you're not at all interested in experiencing pain of any kind, or poly relationships, or married men – say so. (Of course, a percentage of people browsing your profile will pay absolutely no attention to what you're telling them, but at least you can say you warned them.)

You are more than just your kink. If you love to read and write poetry, or rescue animals, or cook gourmet meals, put it in your profile. If you're a comic-loving nerd with a Star Trek uniform in your closet, say so. It gives someone a better idea of you as a complete person, and a complete person has a better chance of attracting someone interested in more than just a casual hook-up.

10 WHAT SHOULD I LOOK FOR IN A DOMINANT'S PROFILE?

Dear Kate:

I've been looking around on FetLife. A lot of the guys I saw on there just had selfies and dick pics. It looked like one of those sites where people go to just find sex!

Any recommendations for what to look for in a man's profile that would be a good sign that they're a real dominant and not just an inexperienced college kid looking for a one-night stand?

- Amanda

Dear Amanda:

Yes, some people are always out there just to find sex, but there is really a core community out there on FetLife that rises above that, more so than any other site I've seen in last decade. Part of this can be seen in the very active discussion groups, where people share experiences, discuss ideas about what it is we do, and sometimes just joke around. They *connect.*

You can usually look at the profile and get a feel for how serious someone really is. If there is nothing there but a photo of their penis, they're probably all about the sex. Worse, they are putting more emphasis on their equipment than what they can do with the total package. The size of the brain is what matters. That's where all the best sex starts.

If they do nothing but talk about how dominant they are, how long they've been a dominant, and how many submissives they have or have had, skip those. If they do nothing but post a shopping list of what they are looking for, skip those too. They are usually assholes just beating their chests. Submissives are people, not pizzas you can order off a menu. Those guys almost never say anything about what they can offer a submissive.

Look for profiles that tell you something about them: not just what they are into sexually, but what they like to read, what music they like, what do they do in their spare time, etc. You want someone you connect with. If you wouldn't want to have lunch with them, you probably wouldn't want to play with them, either.

I'm a sucker for a guy with a sense of humor, who doesn't take himself too seriously. But I absolutely cannot handle someone who doesn't know the difference between "your" and "you're."

See if they belong to any discussion groups, and whether they post anything. Read their responses to see how their minds work. Do they debate civilly, or do they just bluster or resort to insults?

Look at what photos they post to get an idea of what they find arousing. If you find them interesting, then there's a good chance you both have kinks in common. If you're horrified, run away!

(Meanwhile, you should join some discussion groups as well. They are great places to learn and network.)

You will get a lot of messages from potential dominants. If the messages strike you as arrogant or pushy, delete them. Don't waste your time or theirs.

If they give you the creeps, trust your gut. Don't give in to the urge to tell them they are making you uncomfortable. Don't engage with them at all. Just block them.

If their message makes it obvious that they didn't bother to read your profile, ignore them. I get messages all the time from submissive men begging me to do terrible things to them; they are obviously not paying attention to the most basic part of my profile describing me as a collared submissive.

Pay attention to those who are courteous and trying to open a dialogue with you. Give the nice guys a chance.

11 IS IT REALLY IMPORTANT TO READ SOMEONE'S PROFILE?

Mistress Kate:

USE ME AS YOU PLEASE DO HARD DO IT AGAIN AND AGAIN HARDER and harder for as long as you want I am your slave forever I can never wear anything ever again I for I am your slave. Whip me so hard I bleed and squeeze my balls to hear me scream and to stop and don't stop squeeze harder every time I said stop and make sure that I am tired down first and do anything you want to me that you can think of.

*   - slave bobby*

Dear slave bobby:

First things first: I am not your mistress, nor am anyone's mistress. Even if I were a domme with mistress aspirations, I have not yet given *you* permission to address me as such, you disgusting little worm.

It's not that I'm not flattered by your offer. However, as a writer and former English major, I am extremely put off by the poor grammar and lack of proper punctuation. You will make a much better impression on those you wish to serve if you take a little more time and care with your sales pitch.

But even more significantly, however, you apparently failed to read anything at all about me on my website during your visit.

I am a submissive. I do not desire nor seek your submission. Unless, of course, you cook, clean and do yard work. I suspect you do not.

Thanks anyway,

—Kate

12 DO I NEED TO BE TRAINED?

Dear Kate:

I've met this great dominant online that sounds like the real deal. He's been wonderful about answering my questions and giving me his advice on the other dominants that keep messaging me. I was thrilled to have a friend watching out for me.

Now he's offered to be my protector and says he can train me to be a good submissive. But he's given me some rules that make me uncomfortable, like from now on I can't talk to other dominants without his permission, or even other submissives! Part of my training is how to please him sexually, because he says most newbies don't know how to give a good blowjob or how to accept a fisting.

I am really upset about the fisting part, because I told him that was something that scared me and I did not want to do it. But he says I'll never be a good submissive until I learn how to take it, and that no dominant wants a slave that won't do that. He's still being really nice and what he says sounds reasonable sort of, but I still feel weird about it.

Do I need to be trained that way? I've seen on other profiles with a status about "being protected by." Is this what that means?

—Maggie

Dear Maggie:

Guys like him are the reason that I so often sound like a cranky, paranoid kill-joy warning you not to accept candy from strangers on October 31st.

Many dominants are genuinely seeking to share knowledge and to mentor in a non-sexual way; it's a tradition in this community to help newbies as we were once helped ourselves. I've met many wonderful dominants that remain my friends to this day.

But what you've got here is a wolf in a wool sweater, and I can only hope it's really, really itchy. He started out being Mr. Nice Dom and now that he's earned your trust, he's moving in for the kill, suggesting things you don't feel comfortable with. This includes things like meeting him in private; pressuring you for sex acts, either in person or online; asking you not to talk to other dominants; and, my personal favorite, offering to "train" you.

"Training" is one of my pet peeves. There's an entire rant on my website about why submissives do not need to be trained by some "expert." There are no universal standards for how to act as a submissive. Sure, there are some fantasies common to very high protocol relationships — how to kneel, how to carry a drink, how to "display yourself" — but these come entirely from *fiction*. Almost nobody really does it that way, and even the few who do, have their own variations according to what they find pleasing.

An example? Many people will tell you that a submissive should never look a dominant in the eye. They find it disrespectful, as if you are challenging them or acting like their equal. But my own Sir trained me from the beginning to do the exact opposite and *always* look him in the eye. He said he wanted to see my pleasure, my yearning, my pain, my delight; he wanted that intimate connection between us.

Unfortunately I ran into one of those more "traditional" dominants at a party, and when we began to play, I looked him in the eye, all eager obedience. He promptly slapped me hard across the face. I wasn't just physically hurt, I was emotionally devastated. It brought the whole scene to screeching halt. We had not negotiated face slapping as acceptable, and I was still so new I didn't know I needed to. I didn't need someone to train me, I only needed someone to educate me.

What most consider "training" is the learning that you need to do with your master or mistress, because the training itself is part of that bonding process, and only they can prepare you for what pleases them.

When someone offers to mentor or train you, that's generally code for "I want to fuck you without any real commitment to your well-being."

So, no, you don't need to be trained – not unless it's your fantasy to enter that kind of relationship. But I'd still say that this guy doesn't sound like a good candidate for you, if he's determined he's going to shove his fist into your vagina whether you want him to or not.

Any dominant that insists you have to do something you have expressly told him you do not want to do is NOT a dominant. He's an asshole. This is something that you have set as a hard limit. You have every right to say no. At most, a reasonable dominant might ask if it's something you can revisit down the road, or what is known as a *soft limit*. That just means you'll think about it.

And telling you no dominant will want a slave who can't or won't do something? Is he omniscient? Does he personally know every single dominant in the world? It's just not true. A good dominant would not want a submissive or slave to do something they really don't want to do. A good dominant knows that your "yes" only has value if your "no" does as well.

Someone genuinely attempting to mentor you would never, ever ask for sex. That's like a teacher trying to seduce you. It's not ethical. It confuses the power dynamic.

Telling you not to talk to other dominants or other submissives?

Whoa, major red flag! At best, he's staking out his territory, running off other males like a bull in rutting season. At worst, he's one of those abusers who will always try to isolate you from anyone who can offer you support; they want you alone and completely dependent upon them. He wouldn't want you to write to me, either, because I'll tell you he's full of it.

As for the status of "Being Protected By:" in most cases, that is a valid relationship status, thought not necessarily meaning that the protector and submissive have entered into any long-term relationship and rarely is it sexual. Most I know are like big brothers (or sisters) looking out for a kid sister.

I personally don't think submissives need a dominant to protect them; they had better be able to protect themselves. Some do like playing with that fantasy of being a damsel in distress protected by a knight in shining armor. Sometimes a newbie, or someone just out of a relationship or otherwise in a particularly vulnerable state, may seek a dominant they trust to run interference between them and the rest of the world because they know that, for the moment, they need someone watching their back. Sometimes it's purely about keeping a troublesome "suitor" at arm's length.

Chalk this one up to experience, and be glad he showed his true colors before you let him talk you into anything. You were smart to trust your instincts!

13 SHOULD MY DOMINANT ASK FOR MONEY?

Hi Kate,

I am a 41 year-old female and I am stepping in to my first serious D/s relationship. My Sir and I started as a vanilla couple and over the last six months have started with various scenes and play time. We are ready to take it to the next level and he has asked me write him a letter describing the type of submissive or slave I want to be. He asks for 100% submission and has even gone so far as to ask me if I would invest in his business.

When I said "no," he pushed back and said, "I thought you were mine, 100%?"

I do trust him and believe that he definitely has my best interest in mind but I was in a five-year vanilla relationship where I was a "financial slave" and it should have ended much sooner but it took me two years to get back on my feet financially.

I guess I am struggling with wanting to be his property but I don't want to go back to being a financial slave again. It has been challenging for me to train and practice and work on being his very good girl, and then to be told that I must not be his 100% because I don't trust him enough to give him money.

I guess that I just would like to hear from someone with experience as a sub/slave on this. I don't have anyone to talk to about this.

— Liz

Dear Liz:

It's almost easier these days to trust someone with you heart and body than your money. Not just in BDSM, but in any relationship. When I ended a thirteen-year vanilla relationship, I would have bet anything that in separating our assets, my partner would behave as the decent, honorable man I'd always known him to be. I was wrong.

If my master (15+ years now) had ever asked for my wallet, I would have walked. Lucky for both of us that he never did, and I think that's because he understands how important it is for me not to be financially dependent on anyone, or unable to take care of my own financial responsibilities. Does that make me a bad submissive or slave? I don't think so. We are all entitled to our limits, and money is a hard limit for me. It was a hard limit for me even before BDSM, and I don't apologize for it anymore.

There's so much scamming and scandals and theft today, we all have to be cautious. You'd be irresponsible and/or naive not to be.

Some BDSM folk would side with your guy. But then some people say and believe some really stupid things, and keep harping on how things are *supposed* to work, rather than understanding that BDSM has to function in the real world. Total obedience and submission is a *goal* to work toward, not something that can ever be achieved in perfection. Human beings are imperfect; we can never be perfect in anything: not as slaves, not as partners, not as parents. Hell, even vanilla marriages have an escape hatch called divorce.

I think that your gut is ringing a warning bell for you. No one has ever asked me about being expected to invest with his/her master. However, I have seen friends get involved with a partner (dominant, submissive or vanilla) who simply leeched off of them until they had nothing left to take.

You have had a bad experience in the past. You have every right to be cautious.

Does he know about that past financial slavery? If he does, he should be sensitive to your feelings on it. A good master/dominant never asks for more than a submissive is willing to give — because what isn't given with a full and willing heart will fester. If it's not given freely and joyfully is not *given*, it's coerced or manipulated.

He wants your total trust? You have every right to expect his total trust as well. Ask him to let you hold onto one of his credit cards, and see if he trusts you that much.

You have every right to keep finances outside of a BDSM relationship, just as you have a right, for example, to say pedophilia and bestiality are hard limits. It does not mean you are a bad submissive. It means you are not comfortable with those things. It means you are smart and cautious, and if this man doesn't appreciate those qualities, then that says something about him, not you. You wouldn't want an irresponsible and/or naïve master, would you? What kind of master wants an irresponsible and/or naïve submissive? *Only one that is looking to take advantage of her.*

Consider whether six months is really long enough to know whether he's trustworthy. He could be a wonderful man and dominant, but he might be a lousy businessman. Just his asking you to invest makes me uneasy. In your place, I'd consider running a credit check on him, to make sure he's not in debt up to his eyeballs. Because that's what a smart person would do before investing money anywhere with anybody.

I hope this helps. If you are not on FetLife.com you should consider it. There are discussion groups for submissives where you get a lot of feedback from all kinds of people. Some of it is bad, but a lot of it is good, and all of it can help you sort through what you are really feeling.

In any case, I wish you the best of luck whatever you decide.

— Kate

Liz followed up a few days later....

Hi Kate:

Thank you so much for your response. I was reading your book today and it really helped me complete my letter for Him. I described the type of sub/slave I would like to be and the type of Master I would like to have. I used an experience chart similar to the one in your book and sent it to him as well so he would know all my previous experience and what I desire most when it comes to playtime and non-playtime.

We spent about an hour on the phone discussing it and he asked a lot of questions. He listened patiently but stated that in the end what he truly desires is total and complete control. I let him know that I was open to work toward that type of relationship and that it could be a possibility in the future but as it stands right now I have a few hard limits and money is one of them.

We ended the conversation on a bit of an uneasy note but the good thing is that I feel great! The exercise was super helpful for me and the more I thought about it I came to realize that I may not be the right sub for him and he may not be the right Dom for me. I know what kind of sub I want to be and I believe that He, my Master, is out there for me.

- Liz

Dear Liz:

Good for you! I'm glad you've talked honestly with him, and that you're feeling good about it. The right dominant is out there for you. Don't settle.

14 SHOULD I SEDUCE HIS WIFE?

Dear Kate,

I'm fairly new to this all. I've known a man for four years now. He is much older than me, which doesn't bother me, however I do think it has an affect on him. He's also recently married.

He told me last night for the first time he wanted to make me his slave. Is it wrong that I want to be? I'm afraid to ask him "Why now?" We've had sex a handful of times, but it was very basic. I always detected dominance from him in the way he talked to me during and after sex. He's told me on more than one occasion that he is "crazy" about me. And I think I am crazy about him too.

He asked me to seduce his wife. She is vanilla but has hinted to him that she wants to explore with another woman. Should I tell him how badly I want to? He's very honest with me, which is rare and scares me at times. Is it wrong I want to seduce her? Should I even be investing my time into this? Should I stay his slave or run the other direction? I wouldn't want to ruin what he has. Ever.

I don't want to upset him. I'm so confused. Any advice would be appreciated.

Thank you for your time,

- Ellen

Dear Ellen:

I can understand why you're confused; there's a lot going on here, and I'd need more information to even begin untangling this.

The first thing I'd want to know is: what exactly is his relationship with his wife? I have complicated feelings about cheating, because I've been there and done that, and it was one of the most awful things I've ever had to deal with.

Are you comfortable with seeing a man who cheats on his wife? I'm assuming he is cheating, unless they have an open relationship. If they did, I'd expect he would have told you.

I completely understand being attracted to someone in spite of all obstacles, but you have to ask yourself: can I trust him? It is impossible to be a slave or submissive to someone you can't absolutely trust, and here you have a man who is unable to keep the most clear-cut of promises: fidelity.

And to a woman he just *recently* married?

To be a slave or submissive, master or dominant, you both have to be completely honest. His ability to be honest is already in question.

You say he's been honest with you, but really, how would you know? He's telling you what you want to hear, and I know that because he wants to fuck you. A liar always tells the woman he wants to fuck what she wants to hear, and always claims to be honest.

He's lying to the most important person in his life: his wife. She's the one to whom he's made a lifelong, legally-binding commitment. If he will lie to her, he will lie to you. If not already, then in the future. I know how exciting it feels to be his little secret, to feel like he can open himself to you in ways he can't to his wife. I know, I really do. If it's true that he really can say some things to you and not to his wife, it's because he hasn't got anything to lose with you. You are in a little box over here in the shadows; the rest of his "real" life is out there in the open.

You say you don't want to "ruin what he has." He's the one ruining it, not you; but if you go along with this man, that makes you an accomplice. You will feel guilty about this, sooner or later, and guilt is a terrible thing to drag around.

I hope that his request that you seduce his wife is just talk. Do you already know her, and this is why he thinks he might be able to push you both in that direction? Because that is the final straw for me — that he's not just lying to her and cheating on her — but now he

67

wants YOU to make his fantasies come true because he's too chicken-shit to talk directly and honestly to her about branching out sexually. Worst of all, he's plotting to manipulate her into something that she might not actually be ready for, and that could have big repercussions on her life and emotions. It sounds like he wants her to cheat on him to lessen his guilt, or this is just a roundabout way of him trying to get the three-way of his dreams.

Try to think beyond what you want at this moment in time.

Try to think beyond that you don't want to upset him. (Oh, Lord, Ellen! Can you hear yourself?)

Ask yourself what kind of person you are, and what kind of person do you want to be.

Are you just looking for an exciting fling for a week, a month, or a year? Or do you want a long-term open and honest BDSM relationship with someone? If you do, this isn't the guy, and you'll be wasting time, effort and probably a lot of pain in this relationship that isn't going to take you where you really want to go.

Love a cheater, and you spend the rest of your life with him waiting for him to lie to you. At some point, you aren't sure you can even trust him when he says, "I love you."

This is, of course, just my opinion, but maybe there is something here that can help you figure it out.

15 IS IT NORMAL TO FEEL SO NEEDY?

Hi Kate,

I've been married and faithful to my husband, whom I love very much, for more than 25 years. Recently, however, I started having affairs, because our sex life has become almost non-existent because of his health issues.

I found a really nice man who introduced me to his world of dom/sub. In my work and home life, I am the one in charge and the one everyone depends on, so becoming his submissive has been a great relief. I really enjoy taking orders and pleasuring him in every way.

I know for certain I will never leave my husband, but I'm really confused with these feelings that I have for my dom. I'm a very independent woman, and I don't want to confuse it with love. I wait everyday for him to give me instructions on what to wear, whether I can masturbate, or whether I can orgasm. I obey his every command.

Recently he left on a two-week trip, and I felt completely lost. He still stayed in touch everyday, but while at home, he is in constant contact with me. I have to say that I was somewhat jealous of all the time he was spending with someone else. Is it normal to feel this way about someone I've only met four times? Is it normal to develop these kinds of feelings in this type of relationship so quickly?

He has all the signs of a great dominant. We have safe words, and he is taking things very slow with me, introducing new things every time we meet. He's very patient, because I'm completely new to this, but his actions sometimes are very confusing to me. Not sure if this is typical of a dominant, but he can be both very aloof and cold, or, at times, extremely caring and gentle. I'm trying to understand whether I'm going down a destructive path, or if what I'm feeling is completely normal in this kind of situation.

Any insight you can give me would be greatly appreciated.

- Carmen

Dear Carmen:

It is completely normal to feel such an intense connection with a dominant, particularly if this is the first such relationship you've had. BDSM brings together amazing physical pleasure with a strong mental aspect, and the combination is powerful. Add the newness, the joy of discovery and anticipation — and let's face it, for most of us over a certain age, that "fun" kind of anticipation is something we don't experience much anymore. Suddenly, we're like kids on

Christmas morning again, all eagerness and curiosity.

On top of all that, you are experiencing the freedom of being able to let go of the control you have to maintain in your "real" life, and that can be an enormous rush. Instead of having to do the thinking for everyone else, you are able to let someone else take the lead, along with all the responsibility and pressure that go with it.

So yes, it's normal. The dependency, the nearly obsessive need for contact with him, the jealousy.... yep. All normal. It's a roller coaster of highs and lows, thrilling and miserable and joyful and sad and everything in between. After some time, it does tend to level out, which is both good and a little sad in its own way.

As for his alternating aloofness and tenderness, that is something that dominants do, at different times and for different reasons. Some of it is about keeping a submissive in a certain amount of anxiety, because a dominant enjoys seeing his or her power over you. Some of it has to do whatever kind of scene or play is going on at the time, because every playtime is a like a small drama being acted out; he may feel that this particular scene calls for coolness. Some dominants simply see it as a way of making sure you know who is in control.

Sometimes, people are just in different moods due to other pressures in their life. It's possible that sometimes he just doesn't feel particularly affectionate. You say he stays in constant contact, and that says a lot about his commitment to you.

What becomes difficult is eventually you reach that slippery slope of wondering whether it is *just* a good D/s relationship, or is it love? And what is love, anyway?

His different sides may have to do with how he perceives the relationship, i.e. "I am your dominant: not your boyfriend, not your lover, not your husband or your father," meaning that while he may feel affection for you within the D/s relationship, he does not want or intend for romance to be a part of it.

He may be caring as a part of the aftercare after a scene; it's part of his obligation to take care of you in that way, to help you transition back to the real world.

The coolness may be his way of keeping you anchored in "this is not a romantic relationship." It may even be something he needs to do for himself, to keep the relationship balanced. Maybe he is the one afraid of becoming too attached to you. You have a husband you say you have no intention of leaving, and he has other relationships. You both will struggle to balance your emotions.

It's a paradox — and a damned cruel irony — that love often fucks up a good D/s relationship.

You sound well-anchored in your life, and I don't think you're on a destructive path. Unless you find yourself thinking of turning everything upside down to go and live at your dominant's feet 24/7, no matter what the cost, I think you're simply experiencing the normal highs and lows of D/s.

You don't say how long this relationship has been going on. If it's less than a year, then you're still in that sub-frenzy/honeymoon stage that is both heaven and hell.

At this point, it's not all about how great he is or isn't, or whether it's love or not. It's about the new relationship energy, the endorphins and hormones surging through your system, and the thrill of something so new. In the beginning, we fall in love with submission itself, and the way it makes us feel.

Don't do anything rash, and enjoy it while it lasts.

One final comment: are you sure your husband or family isn't going to find out? Are you prepared for what could happen if they do?

16 HOW DO I LEARN TO HAVE AN ORGASM ON COMMAND?

Dear Kate:

I find myself gravitating toward a Dom/sub relationship, which seems so abnormal and insane when I think about it. Yet the very idea is so arousing!

I had one relationship in the past (the most connected I've been able to be with someone) that had some BDSM undertones. At the time I wasn't very aware of the culture and didn't even realize what kind of relationship we had. Now years later at the age of 26, I find myself involved with someone who is experienced in the lifestyle. He was very forthcoming about his sexual dominance, which I was okay with because I'm aware of my submissive nature.

He's been very kind about easing me into things, so I agreed to be his sub/slave. While Sir is willing to answer any questions I have and is very good to me I often feel inexperienced and out of my element.

This isn't something that works well for me considering I am the exact opposite of a sub outside of the bedroom. I want to be knowledgeable and I feel he can only tell me so much because he is a dominant. So he can't really give me a submissive's point of view.

For example, I feel that I'm failing miserably at my orgasm control training. He's been very patient with me but I'm worried he will eventually get tired of being patient. A lot of the info out there is from the dominant's perspective. And I have no idea how to better approach my O training. Is there any advice you can offer?

— Rebecca

Hi Rebecca!

Congratulations on taking control of your life and sexuality.

You are absolutely right that you need more knowledge. Everybody does, because knowledge is power. Power to keep yourself safe, as well as power to grow and expand your horizons.

There is, of course my own book, *How to be a Healthy and Happy Submissive,* available on Amazon as both an ebook and paperback. It contains everything I know about being a submissive and education in BDSM.

I also recommend *SM 101: A Realistic Introduction* by Jay Wiseman, and *Screw the Roses, Send Me the Thorns* by Phillip Miller and Molly Devon. There are a lot of new books out there ever since *Fifty Shades* got soccer moms whispering about BDSM, but not all of them are particularly good. *SM 101* and *Screw the Roses* are excellent, and they have been around since before the *Fifty Shades* hoopla.

Every submissive needs a support network of other submissives. Have you joined FetLife.com? There are a number of submissive discussion groups there that will give you access to advice from thousands of submissives all over the world.

Just remember that not everybody who can type has a clue what they're talking about. But you will find there are a lot of very thoughtful, intelligent people with a ton of experience who are happy to share it with you.

I have to be honest, though, about orgasm control. If you mean being able to "cum on command," I failed at that miserably, too.

Some submissives swear they can have an amazing orgasm just because Master said to, but I find it hard to believe. I know it is possible to "think" yourself to orgasm, and that it can be accomplished with even touching the genitals, but on command? Maybe it happens for some people, but I just don't believe it can happen all the time for the majority of submissives as easily as they say – "they" being all those guys who claim they can teach you how.

But that's my opinion. Now, if you're talking about being able to hold off until given permission, well, that's a different thing. I have been able to do this, but not for very long! Master enjoys hearing me beg and plead and scream PLEASE PLEASE PLEASE!

This is a good kind of question to put out on one of the discussion groups on FetLife, asking other subs what they think about orgasm control and what has worked for them.

Meanwhile, stop beating yourself up. That's his job.

(Let me be clear: that last was a joke.)

17 DO I HAVE TO LET A DOMINANT DEMEAN ME?

Dear Kate:

I've met a lot of dominants online, and there is this one guy who wants me as a slave, not a sub. In the beginning, he promised he wouldn't share me with anybody else, but now has told me he wants to pimp me out for money. He says that if he wants to share me, he will.

I don't want to be demeaned like the videos he keeps having me look at. I told him I wasn't into bisexuality at all. He has already demoted me to cook and housekeeper, with another girl as his sex toy. We also discussed spankings but he wants to use a belt. When I said no, just hand spankings, he said I was too demanding. We haven't even met yet. How can I find a caring dominant?

- Lindsay

Dear Lindsay:

First of all, tell this one to take a hike. Unfortunately, you find a lot of guys like him out there. He's either not "real" or he's an idiot. By not real, I mean he just likes to talk about all this stuff online and probably never has and never will actually *do* anything, so of course he's not concerned with the reality of what you want, or what he has a chance in hell of actually getting. He's getting off on the talk, and your reactions to it.

If he thinks that a dominant is supposed to demand what he wants, and then push and push until he gets it, well, then he's just an idiot. It's always possible he's a little of both.

I love the idea that he has "demoted" you. Exactly how would that work, consider you two have never even met, let alone begun a real relationship?

Don't waste another email on this person; he is so completely not listening to you. The good news is that he has shown his true colors before getting you to meet him in person, where he might have been very aggressive and possibly even abusive.

You have to be patient and keep looking. It's really no different than finding a vanilla lover/partner/spouse; actually, it's harder because you have added to the list of specific qualities you're looking for. But you can find the right one if you're patient and refuse to settle for less than you really want.

- Kate

Dear Kate:

Unfortunately this isn't happening online. This guy is texting me. I know - huge mistake on my part! I am really scared because he is in law enforcement and can really ruin me.

- Lindsay

Dear Lindsay:

Okay, this is getting more complicated and more worrisome. How did you find this guy, or how did he find you? Do you know his real name, or does he know yours? Has he made any threats, specific or otherwise? Is he in your area?

I've known more than one guy who claimed to be a cop; some assholes like scaring people or making people think they are more powerful than they actually are. I suspect that is the case here.

Either block him from your phone or change your number or both. **Seriously, don't talk to him at all from this point forward.**

If he continues to harass you in any way, report him to the police.

In case it comes to calling the police, make a note of whatever details about himself he may have shared. Save those text messages as evidence. I assume you have his phone number? There are services online where you can reverse trace a phone number to find out who he is. I don't recommend this as a means of confronting him

– because you shouldn't do that – but if he continues the harassment, you will need this information.

He is enjoying your discomfort. If he has another girl for his "sex toy" (I don't believe he actually has one for a minute), then he has no reason to keep bothering you, except for whatever cheap bully thrill he gets from making you uncomfortable. Stop giving him what he wants. Don't talk to him.

You've already learned a valuable lesson here. Be very careful about how much information and contact you give someone until you know them better.

I'll keep my fingers crossed that you simply never hear from him again, but please don't hesitate to seek help if you do.

18 AM I MENTALLY ILL TO LIKE THIS STUFF?

Dear Kate:

I have known that I am masochistic for about a year now, and I've been asking a lot of people's opinions on whether or not it is a mental disorder.

My partner at the time got worried and annoyed at my seemingly sudden and unhealthy addiction to pain. We separated, and a few days later, I met my current partner and dominant.

He is the perfect dominant for me, because he is willing to test my limits. But he's been trying to get me to communicate my level of pain more, and use my safe word. The problem is that often I don't realize how bad the injury is and therefore don't try to stop the play. I am enjoying it more than I feel the actual pain. Something might feel like a pinch at the time, but later I've got this huge bruise.

- Tricia

Dear Tricia:

According to the latest reports of the American Psychiatric Association, masochism only becomes a diagnosable dysfunction when *"the fantasies, sexual urges or behaviors cause clinically significant distress or impairment in social, occupational or other important areas of functioning."*

Does this sound like you? If not, then stop worrying.

If you just discovered BDSM activities and found that you enjoyed them a lot, that's not unusual or weird. People who don't understand what BDSM is or how it works, naturally, may think you are doing something unhealthy. Most people spend all their life trying avoid pain, so they don't understand why anyone would seek it out.

We know it's not really about pain, but about sensation. Pain used carefully in an erotic context is very different from a root canal at the dentist's office.

When you say you don't realize how bad it is because you don't feel it, do you just mean that you are having such a good time, it doesn't hurt much? Are you getting that lovely, floaty feeling we call "subspace?"

What you are describing is not unusual. Your body produces endorphins (a hormone in the brain), when you are under prolonged stress (such as play) that produce a powerful natural high. That's why so many people enjoy sadomasochism. It's also why so many religions throughout history have incorporated things like self-flagellation and walking on hot coals into their rituals.

Some submissives can go so deeply into that high – *subspace* – that they have trouble knowing when to stop; some have trouble even communicating at that point. You may simply have a very high tolerance for pain. If any of this describes you, make sure whomever you play with also knows how you react, and is prepared to watch out for you.

If you are having trouble speaking, there are other signals that you can use, like dropping a bandana or toy. The real key here is going slow, knowing your own limits, and having a partner who understands you.

On a completely side note, if you notice you are bruising very easily, make sure you are not diabetic. Diabetics bruise easily and heal more slowly than other people. It doesn't mean you can't play, only that you have to take some extra precautions.

19 CAN I BE HAPPY AS THE SUB ON THE SIDE?

Dear Kate:

I have known for about 10 years I lean towards being submissive but just started my first submissive relationship.

Before we met, he was in a vanilla relationship, and still is. I knew that going in. Every interaction we had is because his girlfriend is not around. He also flirts and has sex with other people, which he tells me about and I am ok with polyamory.

We have an amazing sex life and he has helped me to gain self-confidence and to lose a lot of weight. I know he cares tremendously for a lot of people and gives a lot of himself to others, including his children.

He is in massive debt (more than $35,000 and he has an outstanding lien) and I added him to my cell phone plan and let him use my bank account to cash his checks. He doesn't ask for money directly any more, but has in the past; I have spent a couple thousand dollars on him. I have researched and called people on his behalf and have told him what he needs to do to start working on his debt, but as far as I can tell, he has not acted on *anything I told him. He pays the minimum possible; I figure it will take him 25-30 years to pay the debt off at his current rate.*

I moved away about four months ago to take a new job, and our relationship seems to be getting worse. I pay for all the expenses to see him (airfare, hotel, etc.) and he can only spend 2-4 hours per weekend with me because of his girlfriend. What really hurts is the cost to see him is 50% more for the weekends because of summer price increases, and then he wanted to spend the next three weeks with his girlfriend.

The next weekend is my birthday. He wants me to cancel with my mom, who would come up and spend time with me, so that I can come down and spend the majority of my birthday in airports. I sincerely doubt he would remember or do anything for my birthday; he didn't last year when I was local.

He has been really distant the last three weeks, and as far as I can tell, he has been tired and just hasn't wanted to talk with me. On most days, I might get a couple of texts and maybe a 10-20 minute phone call. Lately, that is about three times a week.

I don't know what to do. I know I want more: ultimately I want a partner, especially in a D/s context, but also someone to grow a life with. I think he wants more of a fantasy, porn life. I know he is depending on my bank account to cash his checks to survive. I know I don't want to be his second/sancha/side ass forever. I know I am emotionally needy, and I need more attention and praise than what he has been giving me. I don't know if he is really into this.

I know in my heart I am submissive. At this point, I don't know if I am being a brat because I want more than what my Master is giving me or if I am in a relationship that is slowly dying.

Any and all insights and advice is very much appreciated. Thank you.

— Elise

Dear Elise:

You are absolutely not being a brat, or a bad submissive. You have legitimate reasons for being concerned.

While you say he has helped you with your self-confidence and health (and probably made a number of your life-long fantasies come true), it seems clear to me that he is getting more out of this relationship than you are.

The monetary issue bothers me a great deal, for a couple of different reasons. The first being the most obvious: that he is taking advantage of you not just through your love and devotion, but through your wallet.

The second is that a man who is not in control of his own life cannot possibly be trusted with control of yours. A good dominant doesn't have to be perfect (who is?) but he does have to have his shit more or less together. This man sounds like a train wreck that is not interested in even trying to put on the brakes.

And excuse me? He wants you to cancel plans with people who

actually love you and remember it's your birthday? Oh, Elise, this man does not deserve you, and you deserve far better.

It is easy to fall hard for the first dominant in your life. It's such a powerful emotional, physical and mental relationship, and our submissive nature wants so badly to please and to be obedient.

But this is where you have to ultimately realize that you have to take care of you. If not for yourself, then at least to preserve and protect yourself for the right master or mistress in your future.

I think you know the answer to this already. A D/s relationship only works when both of you are getting your needs met, and you obviously are not.

It is unlikely that he can give you what you need and deserve. You don't say whether or not his girlfriend knows and consents to his relationship with you, but it is obvious that she comes first. He already doesn't have enough time and attention to give you, but he makes time to flirt and have sex with other people as well? That's not poly, that's being a greedy man-slut.

End this relationship now, and get on with your life. The sooner you do, the sooner you can find what you really want: a lasting relationship where you are loved and valued.

And please, please! Get this man out of your finances before he does serious, long-lasting harm. I'm not sure why he would need your bank account to cash his checks, but it sounds very fishy to me. What is he hiding from his girlfriend that she can't cash his check through her bank account?

I wish you the best. You certainly deserve more than this.

20 WHAT IF MY HUSBAND WANTS ME TO BE HIS MISTRESS?

Dear Kate:

I'm in a hard place. My husband of eight years has been hinting at the fact that he is a submissive, and has been watching porn when I'm not around.

I walked in on him a few days ago, and that's when he told me he wanted me to be his dominant. He was getting turned on just talking to me about it. I just don't think I have it in me.

We have gone over a year and a half without sex because he would always find reasons not to. What can I do? This could break our marriage.

-- Marsha

Hi, Marsha.

Many man have submissive fantasies, and studies have suggested that there are far more submissive men than women out there. Because it is so opposed to the role that society tells them they must play to be "real men," many of them have hidden these fantasies all their lives.

First, keep in mind that we don't choose what arouses us. Your husband didn't get up one day and decide that submissive fantasies of dominant women were going to be his "thing." People have offered lots of ideas about why we are sexually wired the way we are, but no one really knows. We simply are what we are.

Try to be sympathetic that he has shared something so deeply personal and perhaps even embarrassing or shameful to him. Sure, it took him a while to do it, but I know many men who still keep their desires — and activities — a secret from the person who is supposed to know and love them best. He is trusting you not to make fun of him, or be disgusted by him.

What will work in your situation depends on just how submissive he wants to be. Some are thrilled just to have someone who will let them kiss their feet and administer a spanking or two. Some actually like to be denied orgasm for periods, until you give permission. Others, true, do like more involved pain and/or humiliation, but that's not always the case.

Please don't judge by what you see in porn. That is not how it works in real life. You don't have to wear leather and five-inch heels and use a whip to give him what he wants. (Though sometimes a few prop are enough to make his fantasy come true.)

- Talk to him in detail about what it is that turns him on. If necessary, have him write it down. You won't know if you can help him here until you know exactly what he's talking about. Does he want to do this just in the bedroom? Are there specific acts he wants? There are so many different ways a man can be submissive that it's hard for me to speak to all of them.

- There are a number of very good books, and I suggest you read at least one; *Screw the Roses, Send Me the Thorns* is a very good place to start. If you want to know more about dominating men specifically, the best book ever is Mistress Lorelei's *Mistress Manual*. Both are available on Amazon.com, as is my own book, *How to be a Healthy and Happy Submissive,* which may be helpful as an introduction to what BDSM is, though the book is written for female submissives. You'll be surprised at just how many books out there are for just such dominant female/submissive male relationships.

- Start slowly. You say you have not had sex in over a year. Perhaps watching a video or reading a story together will set the mood so that you can at least have some kind of sexual interaction to prime the pump, so to speak. You both need to get reacquainted with each other's body. This hasn't been a good time for you, either, without your sexual needs being met. Trying to meet him halfway could fix that, and I think you'll feel better (at least physically) being touched and pleasured again.

- Start with just a little role-play; mix in things that you would like, too, and see what happens. You owe it to the both of you to keep an open mind and see if you can find some common ground.

- Consider the benefits of this! You have the perfect opportunity to make him happy by getting him to DO WHAT YOU WANT HIM TO. Many submissive men are happy to spend time just massaging their mistress's feet, or performing cunnilingus. If he is truly submissive, you can assign him the household chores! He's offering to give you power, and that could be a very good thing for you, too.

- If all else fails, and you find you just cannot do it at all, consider allowing him to find a professional dominatrix who will allow him to explore without you. Or even with you. She can take charge while you are present as her "assistant."

I know from experience how deep these desires can run. They don't just go away. Please keep an open mind and try to build on this with him. If it works it can bring you both much greater intimacy and trust than you can imagine.

Best of luck!

21 IS THERE A WAY TO TELL IF SOMEONE IS KINKY?

Dear Kate:

There are no BDSM groups in my area, and I'm having a hard time finding a partner. There is a guy I know who really seems like he might be a dominant. Is there some way I can tell if someone is into BDSM?

— Valeria

Hi, Valeria.

It's a tough situation. Unfortunately, there is no secret handshake or code word to find out if someone is kinky or into BDSM. You can drop hints, but there's no guarantee someone will pick them up. You could carry a copy of *Fifty Shades* under your arm to a bar, but an unfortunate side effect of *Fifty Shade's* popularity is a lot of men have found it easy to pretend to be a dominant just to hook-up.

First, are you sure there is nothing in your area? Are you on

FetLife.com? They have a great location page that helps you find both groups and munches in your area, as well as online discussion groups -- and those discussion groups are a great way to forge new friendships and connect with people near you.

There could be a group closer that is just keeping a low profile, and the only way you'd find it would be to talk to people with similar interests. Scan the profiles on FetLife for people in your city or region. A lot of groups may exist under a name you wouldn't expect. Nashville, for example, has a group called "Middle Tennessee Kinksters" as well as a group under the local club name: "CPI/The Mark." Look for possible variations of a group that fits your area.

People who can't always get out in public can still find each other online. With a little common sense and caution, you can find someone that way. That's how I found my Sir more than 15 years ago. We lived in the same city, but I would never have found him if I hadn't looked online.

Look at the profiles from your area. Don't necessarily contact dominants, but look for submissives and ask them if they know of a group. Networking is vitally important, and you can never have enough friends.

Good luck!

22 IS IT POLYAMORY IF HE LIES ABOUT IT?

Dear Kate:

I have read your book "How to be a Happy and Healthy Submissive;" it was so informative and beyond helpful. Thank you for it.

May I ask for some advice?

Something in your book brought the most attention to me though. The dominant I am with now is poly. I asked him how many other subs or how many others is he playing with? He would not give me an answer. I thought in this type of D/S relationship it is to be based on trust, honesty, and openness. Well, I happened to find out the truth one evening. It's not the number of others that is bothersome. It is that he did not tell me himself.

What stood out in your book was when you spoke about the collector dominant. Could you elaborate on this? I did confront him on this issue and it was not received well. I am sorry to bother you but you seem very open and very knowledgeable.

— Donna

Hi, Donna.

Unfortunately, too many people claim to be polyamorous when they don't really understand what it means and aren't really practicing it. They think that being poly is the same as just being in an open relationship (which may or may not be poly, depending on how it is agreed upon by those in the open relationship) or just being a slut. (I don't say slut with judgment, really. Some of my best friends are total sluts. I was one in my younger, wilder days. Now, who has the time or the energy?)

But poly is about loving relationships — not just sex or play — and honesty. If he is not willing to discuss his partners with you, or if he doesn't care enough about his other partners to talk about them with you as an important part of his life, he's not poly. He's just a slut.

Besides what it says about his honesty and openness, the big problem with someone having many lovers besides you is the issue of safe sex. A lot of the poly people I know have very clear rules about who can do what and when with whom -- because they are all sharing fluids and the risk of STDs.

How long have you known this dominant? What kind of relationship do you have with him? Are you just playing, or is it a relationship, D/s or otherwise? If you are in a purely casual relationship, he may not feel he needs to discuss his partners with you. Because of STDs, however, I always feel like someone has a right to ask and be told the truth.

Are you comfortable being with someone who is not being upfront with you?

Without complete honesty, no relationship can work, but especially not D/s and/or poly. Are you willing to put time into a relationship that is always going to have you wondering what he isn't telling you?

23 SHOULD I REPORT MY FRIEND FOR STATUTORY RAPE?

Dear Kate:

As someone in the community can I get your insight? My coworker and friend talks about how he has a dom/sub relationship with his girlfriend. He aggressively cheats on her but I'm guessing that might be part of it, not that it's my business.

The problem is that she is 16 and in high school (and he is 22).

If this was just two consenting adults, I'd just high-five him but this info deeply troubles me. Am I "allowed" to interfere on their arrangement if I feel it is immoral/illegal? Should I contact the police? Is it my business at all? What should I do?

- Martin

Dear Martin:

Wow. That's a tough question because no one ever wants to be the tattletale blowing the whistle on a friend's shenanigans.

However, a sexual relationship with a 16 year-old is more than shenanigans, it's illegal. No way around that. Doesn't matter if the 16 year-old is wise beyond her years with the soul of a 30 year-old, the law of the land says HANDS OFF!

Are you allowed to interfere? Well, yes. Forget the "community," forget dom/sub relationships; this is just plain wrong.

As a teaching point for BDSM relationships, let me point out that informed consent is the cornerstone of what we do. Legally and ethically, you cannot play with someone who cannot give consent — and that's what being "under the age of consent" means — even if sexual intercourse is not a part of it.

Now the question becomes how to approach the situation. Do you know the girl? Do you know her parents? Is this something you could talk to her or her parents about?

How good a friend is this person? If you step in here, are you okay with losing his friendship (please say yes cause he sounds like an asshole)? Consider how you will deal with any blowback from him at work, because that could get icky for you. Be prepared.

Have you tried to talk to him about the fact that what he's doing is illegal?

Anyone can report statutory rape because that is what this is. The state presses charges, not the parents or the girl herself.

You're a good person to be concerned. I hope you are able to find a solution.

24 WHY IS MY DOMINANT'S BEHAVIOR SO UNPREDICTABLE?

Hello Kate:

I am currently in the early stages of a relationship with an experienced D [dominant]. Is it usual that he can be totally dominant sometimes, treat me as a lover other times and sometimes be a combination of the two?

The unpredictability of it is a huge turn on for me, so perhaps that's why he does it. I've talked with some other subs that say their dominant never steps out of role.

I am in no way dissatisfied but I just would like a better understanding of these dynamics, as it is all so new to me. Thanks for your time. You are awesome!

—Grace

Grace:

It's tough to give you advice here, as I'm not seeing your interactions with him. But there are all kinds of dominants, and every dominant sees his/her relationship in a slightly different way. Submissives are the same way.

Many dominants do not maintain a strictly dominant attitude, but then it depends on what you think (and what they think) a "dominant attitude" is. Some dominants are into "high protocol" —a lot of rules about how you both behave — but in my experience, many more are not. It's tough to be "in role" all the time; sometimes they just want to relax as much as we do.

The only thing to be concerned about is if he is so unpredictable that it confuses you. If, for example, he says very casually, "Hey honey, can you bring me a soda while you're in the kitchen?" And then when you do, he smacks you across the face for not bringing it to him naked on your knees. Does that make sense? It's one thing to be spontaneous; it's another to be unfair.

Generally I'd say if you enjoy it, and he enjoys it, it's okay. Many dominants step out of role, as do submissives. It doesn't mean that they aren't good doms/subs or that they aren't serious about it. It depends on what kind of relationship they are building together.

Consider that both dominants and submissives have to flexible and adaptable if their relationship is to last. Life doesn't always let us live out our fantasies the way we'd like.

If, as time goes on, you become less turned on by his behavior and more confused, talk to him about it. Never, ever be afraid to tell him what you are feeling or to ask for clarification. Besides the fact that communication is essential to a D/s relationship, many submissives believe that all their thoughts and feelings belong to their dominant; to hide something from him or her is a serious violation of a submissive's surrender. Neither of you can meet the other's needs if you don't know what the other wants.

25 AM I TOO ALPHA TO BE A SUBMISSIVE?

Dear Kate:

I am not a submissive and because of my Alpha personality, I do not know that I ever could be. But there is a huge part of me that wants to experience it. I would love to have my boyfriend and I experiment in and learn some things as an option in our sexual arsenal.

I am a control freak in my daily life because of my job, and I am also a full-time single mother, so I am basically in control of absolutely everything 24/7. I have always found the concept of being submissive and having someone else take control so appealing, but I am not entirely sure I know how to approach this with the guy that I am dating or where we would go to learn.

I have an exceptional interest in being bound; the idea of having enough trust in someone to immobilize me and knowing that I cannot do anything except experience pleasure is such an incredible thought.

My other issue is that I am NOT a small girl at all. I am almost 5'10" and am over 200 pounds. I wear a size 16 jeans so I tend to be a little bit self-conscious and that prevents me from being able to cut loose as much as I really want to. I am in the process of attempting to get more exercise and eat

better but sometimes it is hard to do so.

I guess I am just asking if you think that this is just some kind of

curiosity thing that I will be able to satisfy just by continuing to read up on

it or if this is actually something that I should try to further explore.

—Kim

Dear Kim:

First of all, what you are describing is not the least bit unusual. With everyone except my Sir (and sometimes even with him!), I am very much an Alpha myself. There are many strong, independent women (and men) who enjoy some level of submissive precisely because it does allow them to finally let go and simply be in the moment without having to be in control of it. I don't know if you've read *Fifty Shades of Grey*, but in the real world, Christian Grey is far more likely to enjoy being a submissive than a dominant.

There are also people who consider themselves "switches" because they enjoy doing both. Sometimes they are the dominant partner, and sometimes they like being the submissive partner.

A lot of people think that submission and dominance have to be somehow permanent, inflexible decisions that describe you twenty-four hours a day, seven days a week. For a small percentage of people, it is, but far more people use D/s (dominance/submission) as something to spice up their relationships, that they engage in only on "date nights" or when the kids are out of the house. There is absolutely nothing wrong with a little role-play just to have fun.

You can enjoy bondage without being a submissive at all, though it certainly enhances the experience. There are people who enjoy doing a lot of things associated with submission — bondage, spankings, etc. — without ever giving up any of their personal power. They just like doing that particular activity. That's what is known as "bottoming."

Should you try to explore this? Definitely! You don't want to be ninety years old on the porch of the nursing home thinking, "You know, I wish I'd tried X, Y and Z back then."

Talk to your boyfriend about it. Just tell him you read something or saw something and was thinking it might be hot to be tied up and teased. He'll probably like the idea. He might even say, "Cool! Can you tie me up afterward?"

My only concern is that you do it SAFELY. Rope bondage can be tricky, because there are a few right ways to tie someone up and lots of wrong ways. You want to make sure that you or your partner tie a knot that is easy to untie in case something unexpected happens. Even if you are tying a "safe" knot, get a pair of EMT scissors and keep them nearby, just in case you get a muscle spasm or a panic attack or your mother shows up at the front door unexpectedly. Don't use handcuffs; they are uncomfortable, people always lose the key, and they can cause nerve injury if used for extended periods.

An even better option is a nice soft set of ankle and wrist cuffs. You can adjust them to fit you, and attach them with a carabiner to a rope tied to the bed. Easy on, easy off; you can buy them online or at the local adult bookstore. If you enjoy that, you can get a book on bondage that shows how to tie knots, if you want to go that far.

There are lots of books out there that can give you hints on how to talk to your boyfriend, how to tie knots, all the ways you can role play and experiment. In fact, I just wrote one. Mine is especially slanted toward how to begin exploration and how to find your local kinky community to learn more in person from experienced kinksters.

But you can also try Jay Wiseman's *SM 101*, or his specifically bondage book (though that might wait until later, it might be a little much for beginners) or Dr. Gloria Brame's *Come Hither*.

Now, about your size: I'm 5'1" and extremely curvy. I understand being self-conscious, believe me, but life is too short to let it stop you from enjoying yourself. Don't be intimated because all the books and movies show these skinny little Barbies doing this stuff. In real life, all ages, shapes and sizes do this and have a damned good time.

I wish you the best of luck!

26 HOW DO I APOLOGIZE TO MY DADDY?

Dear Kate:

I am a very new sub, like first time w/a Dom. I got so overwhelmed with the BDSM aspect, I took and took from my daddy and I know he is taking on other subs (which is fine).

However, he has told me he is spent and has no fuel. I really screwed up and did not try to approach him from the human aspect of who he is to try and recharge him. Totally messed that up.

When he tried to tell me what I was not doing, and how I was not showing the same passion and tenacity being intuitive to him as a person, I argued and tried to talk my way out. I was disrespectful trying to "make my point" and we argued.

I am trying to clean the slate, but I am not sure it is going to work. He says text, talk and pics are not going to get it, and when I said I would come to see him (1st time) he said, "And what would we do?"

My response was: talk, be together, watch tv; I would bath and wash him and rub him down and try to help, and that was not what he wanted to hear. He said I would know if I had been paying attention.

I don't know what to do. I am afraid if I ask what I should do, he will be very upset, as I should know. This is my first daddy; I will be so upset if I screwed this up.

— Sonya

Hi, Sonya:

I am sorry you are in pain right now, but I'm not sure what I can tell you that might help. I don't know exactly what is going on, and I don't know either you or your daddy. You say this is your first time as a sub, and you haven't actually met him yet? This is all online?

Have you done any serious reading up on what BDSM is, and how the relationship between a dominant and a submissive works? It's a give and take, each of you making sure the other's needs are met. It sounds as though he feels his are not.

I try to be respectful of online relationships. I know they can be very intense, and many insist they are just as real and valid as any real time relationship. I can understand that to a point; I myself really got to know my own Sir through long, long periods of chat on the internet. But it then progressed to real time, and that is when the relationship of Dom/sub really started. I must be honest: I just don't see how an online relationship in terms of BDSM can work. To me, BDSM is intensely "hands-on" and fed by physical intimacy.

But online or real time, don't be afraid to ask him what you can do to make amends. You fear upsetting him, but honest communication is the only way any relationship can survive. He needs to tell you what he wants, because he can't expect you to be a mind reader. A dominant is supposed to help you learn how to please him. You are supposed to pay attention; serving and pleasing him should be what you desire most.

You admit you've been disrespectful, and that is a very, very bad thing. A submissive can disagree with the dominant, but should always present his/her thoughts in a respectful way. A submissive should always honestly analyze their own behavior without ego or trying to make excuses. Ego — the desire to be right, to get the last word — these are things a submissive must let go of.

So begin with a sincere, humble apology and leave out any excuses. Apologize for your disrespect, and for not being more attentive to his needs. Ask him if he will consider helping you know exactly what it is that he wants and needs from you, and give you the opportunity to do better.

It sounds as if you both need better communication and negotiation about what you expect from each other, and how to provide it. Please consider doing some studying up on D/s relationships to be sure this is what you want and that your expectations are realistic.

I hope you are able to work this out and move forward.

27 HOW CAN A BISEXUAL MALE FIND A DOMINANT?

Dear Kate:

I'm a mature bisexual submissive bottom guy, searching hopelessly (so far) for a dominant master to discipline and use me. I live with my vanilla female partner who knows nothing of this side of me. Am I unreasonable in wanting to find a regular arrangement to satisfy my needs as a sub, whilst maintaining my "normal" vanilla life?

At any rate, I don't seem to be able to find any candidates for the role of master - never mind not accepting the first one that comes along! I can't really go to public meetings (munches or whatever), as it would be impossible to conceal this from my partner. I have registered on many contact sites, but the majority of people on these sites are not true doms. On BSDM.com, I even paid for a month's membership, and messaged several of the (few) people advertising in my area, but had not a single reply. I'm a member on FetLife, and have hardly any success contacting people on there, and nothing that has come to fruition.

Am I just very unlucky to be living in an area of the UK devoid of possible matches, or are my requirements just too difficult or unreasonable to have any chance of success?

— Mike

Mike:

I'm sorry that you've had no luck in finding what you want. It's frustrating, I know. You are not at all unreasonable in wanting to find what you need. I do, however, see a couple of obstacles.

The first obstacle: you mention "mature." I don't know how old you are, but I am fifty-four myself, and the sad reality is that many of the people out there looking for play partners or even just fuck buddies spend most of their time running after much younger partners. While I have been collared to my master, Beast, for 15+ years, we are polyamorous. I wouldn't mind another playmate, but there aren't a lot of men out there looking for fifty year-old women. Some, yes, but not nearly as many as are even now filling the email boxes of twenty-four year olds with far fewer brain cells than me.

(Sorry, that was meant as a joke, but came out kind of snarky, didn't it?)

The second obstacle: you feel you cannot get out and meet people. I don't judge your reasons for this, but that makes it hard to really get to know people. The good masters out there really want more than just emails and profiles; they want a chance to interact with you in person. Making friends with similar interests is a very important part of the networking that leads to finding the right partner or master.

It may put some people off that you don't go out to events or munches, and want to keep this secret from your vanilla life partner. They may get the impression that either you're just one of those guys who wants a little something on the side, and that you aren't seriously interested in building a real D/s relationship.

When I first started in this lifestyle, I thought I was a switch. I have dominant and sadistic tendencies, and so I sought out submissive male partners. But what I found overwhelmingly were married or committed men who weren't really interested in submitting to me or anybody; they had very specific fantasies they wanted to act out, and they just wanted me to follow the script in their head.

Now, there's nothing wrong with wanting to experience certain things, like being fucked by a woman in a strap-on, as long as you are up front about what you really want. They didn't want to submit, they wanted kinky sex. I became really frustrated with men who had no interest in all in what I might want from them, and no interest in surrendering any of their power to me. What they really wanted was a hooker with a whip.

I mention all this because you may need to consider what message you put out there with your profiles and emails. Are you really interested in submitting to someone, or do you just want kinky sex with a man? Be honest. Good dominants that are serious about D/s don't want to waste their time if they aren't sure you are really interested in submission. Among women, we read any mention of "discreet" as "married" and, therefore, no chance of a real relationship.

Then there is the issue of keeping it secret. I understand, I really do, about wanting to keep your "normal" life separate and safe. I tried that myself. It was a complete mess. There is a special circle of hell for cheaters, and I've been there. I don't want to ever do it again.

People who are serious about D/s believe in honest and open communication. If you are lying to your vanilla partner, they often don't trust you to be honest with them.

You say you have had little success with contacting people on Fetlife. Are you just sending out emails asking for partners? Or are you participating in group discussions and trying to form some actual friendships? You need to do that. Fetlife is about social networking, not just a site for hookups.

I don't know about your area of the UK, but generally, there are kinky people all over. Tonight, I went to a local shop to have something printed, and ended up having a long conversation with the woman who took my order; it turns out she used to be a pro domme.

I don't know if any of this has been helpful. I hope that you find what you are looking for. I know what it is to want it. Think about my suggestions, but you may also want to find a bisexual male who has been successful in finding a master, and ask him if he would just give you some advice on approaching possible partners. There may be aspects to homosexual and bisexual D/s I just don't know about. If you are approaching gay men, they may be put off by you being bisexual, because there are still people who think bisexuals are just confused about their orientation. (I know this isn't true, but there are those who believe it, just as many kinksters think switches are equally confused.)

Be patient and keep trying, but consider trying to make some friends among kinky folks all over, not just ones you hope to have a relationship with. Friends with whom you can discuss these things help a lot, and you need advice specific to submissive and gay/bisexual males that I just don't have. You can make safe, anonymous friends online from whom you can seek advice.

I wish you the best of luck. Consider talking to your vanilla partner. She may surprise you.

Hello Kate:

Thanks very much for a very full reply.

Just a couple of points. My age - late fifties - and I'm sure you're right about the preference for younger people, although I suspect it's less of an issue for those seeking a male sub than a female. In any case, my experience has been that there's a far higher proportion of subs and bottoms amongst older guys, than younger, so I suppose that means more competition. For what it's worth, I'm really only interested in men in or near my own age group, and although I like women of all ages, I very much prefer older.

I think you've hit the nail on the head when you identify people who, rather than wishing for a purely submissive relationship, are actually looking to follow a script. This is a very good description of me, and I'm grateful for your insight into the distinction between the two things, which hadn't really occurred to me. However, whilst it may be helpful, maybe cathartic, to become aware of that distinction, it doesn't get me any closer to finding what I'm looking for. In a way, it makes it even more difficult, because as you point out, a true dom(me) isn't going to be interested in someone whom they regard as just "playing at it," and someone who isn't a true dom(me) has to be a consummate actor to be able to give a performance of the script convincing enough to satisfy! I suppose the key point here is that I'm not looking at submissiveness as a lifestyle I want, but rather as an occasional sexual experience. It's obviously not the same thing, but is it a hopeless ambition?

All of this makes me sound very selfish, and obsessed apparently with getting what I want. Maybe it isn't possible to find anyone who can run that script convincingly, and get pleasure from it themselves; if they're a true dom(me), they want the real thing, and if they aren't, they won't enjoy it.

As to the issue of cheating, I don't really know how to handle that. I believe that a frank admission of my preferences would end any sexual relationship with my partner, and there's little enough of it as it is. In a way, I justify it to myself, on the grounds firstly that I'm seeking something she can't give me, and secondly that it poses no threat to the relationship. I have no desire or intention to leave her. I'm painfully careful about identity, communication, accommodation, etc., and as a consequence always have an easy mind when she's around, because I know there is no risk of exposure. The corollary of that is, of course, that it's much more difficult to meet people than it would be if I could come and go as I pleased and anywhere I liked.

Regards, and many thanks

—Mike

Mike:

I don't think you are selfish at all; we all want what we want, and we have a right to want satisfying sex. It's just a tricky matter sometime finding a partner whose desires mesh with our own.

Being aware of the distinction — that you aren't looking for so much of a submissive relationship but more about occasional role-play — may actually help you in communicating what you actually want. I don't mean to dismiss anyone as "playing at it," it's just a variation in wants and needs. The frustrations in my dominant forays were due to men not understanding that when they claimed to be submissive, I expected something from them that they never wanted to give in the first place. Neither of us was right or wrong, real or "playing" – we just weren't on the same page.

I do believe that someone out there would enjoy that occasional role-play with you. But as you well know, it's a problem to find them. Maybe describing it as seeking role-play will better focus your search. Don't say you're looking for a dom/me, but a top.

Some female dominants make a living providing professional services precisely because so many men want to experience some level of submission/bottoming, while keeping it discreet and free from emotional tangles. If you are willing to try a pro-domme, she would be able to give you at least some of what you're looking for. A pro might also have contacts among other bisexual male clients who would be open to joint playtime.

I still think you're going to have a hard time finding partners if you can't go out and meet people, and that you need to find another male with similar desires who can give you advice better tailored to your situation.

I do wish you good luck. Don't give up. :)

28 HOW DO I KEEP MY BRAIN OUT OF THIS?

Dear Kate:

I am a married woman for 18 years. I have recently reconnected with an old boyfriend who is a dominant. I have always wanted to be submissive, but never have explored it.

The old boyfriend has asked me to be his submissive and I have accepted. THEN my brain takes over and I lashed out....

I have since made amends but am reduced to slave now. He has expressed he still has feelings for me and has said he loves me.

How do I keep my brain out of this?

— Lisa

Hi, Lisa.

Are you still married? I understand, because I've been there, done that and have the divorce to prove it. There's a 90% chance you will be found out. Make sure you are willing to accept the consequences.

I'm not sure what you mean when you say your brain took over. There can be a lot of reasons you might get nervous. Could it be because you're anxious about cheating? Or is it really about the submission? Getting nervous and reacting with anger, harsh words, backing out, changing your mind -- all of these things are not unusual. It's scary taking these first steps.

You don't say whether this is online or in real time, if you've actually done anything or just talked about it. Does this old boyfriend have any actual experience with BDSM? If not, and you proceed, you both need to read up on BDSM. I suggest Jay Wiseman's *SM 101*, and my own book, *How to be a Healthy and Happy Submissive.* Both are available on Amazon.

No one can "reduce you to a slave." That's not how this works. Your dominant can be disappointed in you; he can express that, and he can even punish you within the boundaries you BOTH agreed to in the beginning (you might agree to hand spankings, but not with a belt, for example).

But "slave" and "submissive" are really just words. He can call you a slave, which for him may mean you've disappointed him so he will treat you more like property and less like a cherished pet, but whether you are slave or submissive is something you have to agree to.

You can't leave your brain out of this. Sorry. You can overcome your fears — if they are irrational fears — but worrying that someone will really hurt you, worrying that your heart will be broken, worrying that your husband will find out: these are things you can't and shouldn't turn off. Those things will only be lessened as you build trust with this person, and confidence in yourself.

Only you can give yourself permission to let go and follow this path to see where it leads. You have to know that you really want this, and it sounds like you do. But you also have to know that you've chosen someone you can trust to travel that path with you.

Good luck. Be safe. Have fun.

29 CAN I SERVE TWO DOMINANTS AT THE SAME TIME?

Mistress Kate:

I am a 45 year-old guy from Texas. I have met a couple who are both dominant. I have been a submissive to a master before, but I worry that being a sub to two demanding adults may become more of a challenge than a pleasure.

I am bisexual so servicing the master at the mistress' command is not an issue. But just wondering what you think of me being a sub for both.

—Carlos

Hi, Carlos:

First of all, you should not address me as "mistress," as I am a submissive like you. I realize that I often sound like a dominant, so I'll forgive you this time. <smile> I know you are just trying to be polite.

It's impossible to say whether being a sub to both will be a good thing or a bad thing. It depends so much on what they are like as dominants, and what kind of submissive you are.

I've known such situations to work out wonderfully. If they have a good relationship, and they are both on the same page regarding their relationship with you, then I'd say, give it a shot.

You don't say whether you'd be living with them or separately and serving only for short periods. Naturally you'd want to be much more cautious about moving in with them. Living with them would be more demanding, naturally, and more complicated to end the relationship if it doesn't work out.

How good do you feel about they way they communicate with you? Do they listen when you have questions? Have they spelled out their expectations of you? How well do you know them? Do you know other people who have played with them before?

Make sure you've been honest about your concerns, and see how they respond. If you don't see any red flags, I say go for it!

Have fun, and be safe.

30 WILL BDSM RUIN "REGULAR" SEX FOR ME?

Dear Kate:

I'm feeling pretty lost. After playing at it for months, reading online, reading erotica, having sex that feels so meaningless and unexciting and faking orgasms because I know they won't make me cum, I am pretty sure I'm submissive and a rope bunny.

But I'm scared because I feel like it appears in all aspects of my life. I roll over to my guy friends who are demanding and tell me to do things, but because when someone tells me to do something with conviction and commanding in their voice, I sincerely want to do it for them even if later I realize I shouldn't have.

I really want to jump into the world of BDSM but I'm scared it's going to ruin regular sex for me, that I'm going to be not normal, I worry that it's going to take over my life and I'll completely become a push-over. I don't want to lose who I am. It doesn't help that none of my friends are into it (I'm only 20 and in college).

I joined FetLife but I'm too scared to go to a munch alone, even though I want to and because it makes it way too real.

—Olive

Hi Olive:

First, let me assure you: exploring BDSM is not going to ruin "regular sex" for you. Just because you become a gourmet cook doesn't mean you won't still enjoy the occasional burger and fries. It sounds like regular sex isn't doing it for you anyway, so what have you got to lose?

But you bring up a very important thing to consider: in your fear of becoming a total "push-over" is the question of whether in opening yourself to submission, you can still make good decisions to protect yourself, physically and emotionally. It's good that you're self aware enough to admit that you may have made some bad decisions in the past because of your desire to please.

Unfortunately, I think this is true of just about every submissive I've ever met. Throughout our lives, that desire to please and obey has been there, but is it something that we control or does it control us? Can we balance what we desire with being a competent adult?

We have to ask ourselves *why* we do it. Do we do it because we're weak and unsure of our own judgment, or because it makes us feel good and feeds that part of our soul that longs to serve? It's vitally important to make sure we're drawn to this lifestyle for reasons that will fulfill and empower us, not out of fear, abuse, or desperation.

When you come to BDSM in weakness, you'll find yourself easy prey for those who will only exploit your broken parts and make it even harder for you to trust yourself and know your own value as a part of creation.

Some of us have felt broken and incomplete in "vanilla" society because there is something deep inside us that is simply different. Not bad, not "wrong," just *different* from the path most people choose to tread. Our needs run deep and wind through the very core of us. Until we confront those needs, and embrace that difference, we will always feel that something is missing.

If you are one who hungers for the "right" reasons, just knowing that there are others who feel similar things will help you feel more comfortable in your own skin.

I say "right" reasons for lack of a better term. Some have been so battered and twisted by their lives that they have come to loathe themselves, and seek pain, humiliation and degradation because they feel they deserve no better. They come to believe that if they will let people do terrible things to them, or if they are "good" enough in blind obedience, then finally someone will give them the love they so desperately crave. Or they fear that if they don't do what other people want, the love they do have will be taken away. This isn't healthy, and not a "right" reason for giving your body and soul to another.

But which came first? Yearnings for things you didn't understand that made you feel "broken?" Or bad experiences and people that "broke" you, so that then you began to think submission, pain or servitude was either what you deserved, or the only way you could earn love? In other words, did submission become a default survival behavior, not a choice?

Even if we are not a survivor of some enormous trauma, just about all of us have some weak spots that we need to protect.

Early in my life, I recognized in myself this enormous capacity for devotion, to give myself -- physically and emotionally -- to someone with an intensity that could rarely be reciprocated. And with each failure, I felt worse and less loveable. If I was willing to give so much, I wondered, why could they not accept it? I felt as if I were running after people, desperately trying to give them a beautiful gift that they would not even open. Or if they did, they did not recognize what was inside, how lovely and complex it was.

I became a bit of a bitch to compensate, unwilling to completely open myself to others because my submissive nature made it so easy for even well-meaning friends and lovers to hurt me deeply. I wondered what was wrong with me. Why did I need to give so much, and why I was getting so little in return? My life as a submissive and slave has taught me that I simply am wired differently, and that level of devotion and obedience in me is not wrong or bad or unnatural, it was merely a facet of my personality looking desperately for the right person to give itself to.

Like many others, I always had dark fantasies that made me wonder what was wrong with me. But my sense that something was "wrong" with these fantasies was tied to the seemingly opposite knowledge that I did not deserve to be treated this way. I knew I was intelligent, witty, caring, capable and responsible, a good and decent person. So why on earth did I want all those "bad" things?

Finding the lifestyle community gave me the valuable insight that I was not the only one who'd ever felt such yearnings. I learned that the things submissives want are not bad in and of themselves: kneeling or crawling is not bad, if done for the right reasons, in the right time or place, with the right person. Sex is not bad. Licking someone's boots is not bad. Being flogged or whipped is not bad; the right or wrong is all in the context and the consent. I was able to shed so many of the restrictions and norms that society imposes on us, to examine these acts in a objective light, to find out how I felt, not what everyone told me I should feel. There is enormous power in that.

For submissives, our natural urges to give service, devotion and obedience to someone who earns it (not just anyone, but someone who earns it by treating us with respect, care, compassion and understanding) are a bright and shining thing to be treasured.

But those things also need to be protected. How can you do that? First of all, do more reading of non-fiction on BDSM, particularly the dominance and submission aspect. I recommend the following:

- *SM 101: A Realistic Introduction* by Jay Wiseman;
- *Screw the Roses, Send Me the Thorns: The Romance and Sexual Sorcery of Sadomasochism* by Phillip Miller and Molly Devon
- *The Master's Manual: A Handbook of Erotic Dominance* by Jack Rinella
- *Different Loving: The World of Sexual Dominance and Submission* by William Brame and Gloria Brame

If you are now signed up on FetLife, join some of the discussion groups for submissives. Making friends among other submissives is the best thing you can do for yourself as you start this journey, and you can talk about all these feelings with others who feel the same. Do it online if a real-time munch is too scary right now. You might even be able to find the people who hold those munches through Fetlife; getting to know them a little by chatting online will help you find the courage to join the party.

Most of all, go slow. Be patient. There is no prize for getting to the finish line, there is only the pleasure of the ride. Savor it.

31 SHOULD A SUBMISSIVE BE INFORMED THAT THEY ARE BEING TESTED?

Dear Kate:

Recently, I met a dom online and we dated for two months before we had intimacy. I am very new to BDSM so I was also looking for Him to train me as a slave. As my Master and I do not meet often, my task was to send him a sexy pic of myself every morning before 9 a.m. which I have been religiously doing so.

We had our first intimacy without protection last week and I found out that I had an infection. Given that I met my Master online, I had not really done any proper checks and we both assume we are clean. So when I visited the clinic, the doctor suggested I do a STD test. The results will be out next week.

While I was going through this, I continued to submit my pictures to him. However, after our intimacy last week, my Master stopped replying all my messages. He was unreachable for three days, and I had no clue why. I wanted to tell him what I was experiencing and I was scared, but I couldn't locate him. I texted him many times, and eventually I was exasperated I sent him an angry text just to see if he would reply me. He finally responded.

He told me the silence of three days was a test that I failed miserably. I didn't play my role as a sub to please him, rather I accused him of passing STD to me. I had totally no clue I was being tested, his disappearance just felt like I was being used and dumped.

I read about doms testing their subs from different sources. Some sites say submissives need not be informed when they will be tested, while some sites disagree with that as submissives might misconstrue the silence as the end of the relationship which in my case, I had indeed had this thought. I understand that before the test, the subs ought to be informed that they will be put through a test and is assured that this doesn't mean the end of the relationship.

Now I am very confused. I do not know if I am a lousy sub as I became exasperated for attention or could my Master have informed me about the test before he went out of contact.

Can you share your views with me please? And how can I get him back, he is so angry with me he isn't talking to me right now. Is there any way I can punish myself to show him that I am repentant?

Regards,

—Sandra

Hi, Sandra.

I have two distinct reactions to this, and I'm honestly not sure which to give you. Sometimes a dominant isn't testing, he's being an asshole. But sometimes a dominant doesn't respond the way we would like for a good reason.

A good dominant should care about the well being of his or her submissive. I have my doubts about any dominant who would have the first intimacy with you, and then fall silent, and then he's not concerned about your fears of an STD? He should be just as worried as you about the possibility that one or both of you may have a sexually transmitted disease.

Please insert my soapbox rant regarding unprotected sex. Safe, sane and consensual, remember? There's a reason SAFE comes first. A thump on the head to you both for being careless. A smart person takes care of themselves; a good submissive takes care of her master/mistress' property.

But let's back up a minute. How firm was this relationship to begin with? You call him your master, but has he said he accepts that level of commitment? Too many people throw around the title of master/mistress as cheaply as Mardi Gras beads.

I ask this because it totally changes my advice here. If this was an online relationship of a few weeks that finally came to a meeting with unprotected sex, then it sounds to me like you've been, as you suspected, "used and dumped."

This happens a lot, in both the vanilla and kinky world. You meet someone online, there's a lot of talk, then you agree to meet.... A story as old as Adam and Eve.

On the other hand, maybe this man had honest intentions of beginning a relationship, but your reactions made him reconsider. It's impossible to tell at this point, and you'll never know.

As a submissive, we must honestly (brutally!) examine our actions, emotions and motivations, and that is why I am playing devil's advocate here. You say you had an infection. What kind of infection? Because the doctor suggested an STD test, it sounds like this infection was not an STD but more along the lines of a yeast infection. If that is the case, then I think you overreacted.

The doctor was wise to suggest an STD test, considering that you're having unprotected sex. Why on earth would you assume you both were clean?

I totally understand getting nervous; suddenly you realized you were playing Russian roulette. Maybe you panicked a little.

Or maybe, just maybe, you were hurt that he wasn't responding, and thought this was a good excuse for getting angry and insisting he get back to you?

Your complaint about being tested without being told you were being tested sounds a little petulant.

When you are serving a dominant, practically *everything* is a test of some sort. We are always striving to please and obey, so every command – or even the absence of one – is a task to be accomplished with as good grace as we can manage.

While your feelings are completely understandable, your reactions were not those of a good submissive.

Even if a dominant is being an asshole, a submissive does the best he/she can to uphold their end of the bargain of submission until such time as it becomes clear the dominant is not behaving honorably. There could have been perfectly reasonable explanations for his silence for three days: a lost or broken phone; a family emergency; insanity at work.

Was he wrong to leave you hanging with no response at all? I think so, given the recent sexual contact. But I also think you behaved… well, maybe not badly but not well either.

Dominants absolutely do not respond well to demands for attention, and the more aggressive a submissive gets, the more it stiffens their resolve to show you who is in charge. (This is why being a dominant is such a hard role to fill; it's tough to know when to teach you which lesson, and how to do it.)

Think carefully about this relationship. Do you believe he is as invested in it as you are? Is it possible you got caught up in the thrill and thought it meant more than it did? How do you feel about him now that this has happened?

You are looking for someone you can trust, who will help you grow and learn and experience. But you need to pick the person to whom you give your devotion carefully. If you haven't laid a firm foundation for a real, thriving relationship, don't be surprised when you're treated like a one-night stand.

If you want to salvage this relationship, then compose a simple letter of apology. Leave out the excuses, leave out blame, leave out any justifications. Say you realize you were wrong to push him, that you were too hasty in jumping to the wrong conclusions, and that you hope he will forgive you.

How he reacts to this will tell you a lot. But frankly, I'd start over, and go more slowly this time.

Two words of warning, though:

1) Be careful about sending pictures to anyone. I am hoping these did not show your face. Remember that once something is on the internet, it never goes away. Never. It is always out there.

2) Be safe. Use a condom. This is your life we're talking about.

I wish you the best of luck. Keep your chin up.

32 CAN I BE SUBMISSIVE WITHOUT SERVING SEXUALLY?

Dear Kate:

I would like some advice. I am a male who tends toward the submissive side of the spectrum, but I am not into BDSM. I've been told I would be what is considered a "soft sub."

I do not wish to be a slave and I don't really want a traditional domme. I like being told what to do and receiving praise when I obey. I like to be told no and apologizing. I want to be emotionally naked and to feel safe and protected. I think I would describe the situation I seek as a cub with a momma bear.

Does anything like this exist? The only thing I find when I look up dominant women is more extreme forms of dominance.

I'd appreciate any advice you can offer me.

—Donnie

Dear Donnie:

While certain types of BDSM get all the attention (because they make sensational fodder for news, movies, TV and porn in general), just about anything you can think of exists somewhere in the kinky world.

You say you are not "into BDSM" but that's because you've only seen the tip of the iceberg. If you are submissive —you like being told what to do, and being praised for it — then you are into BDSM.

The confusion comes in because BDSM is a generic umbrella term; it encompasses many kinds of kink. You can be into only one kind of kink, or you may combine several or even all of them. A person can enjoy bondage, but not be a submissive at all, for example. Another might enjoy all kinds of things, but not want to play with any kind of pain.

You are not interested in the physical aspects of play, either pain or pleasure, but only in the service and mental aspects, and that is perfectly okay. You are not alone in this. There are as many different ways to engage in BDSM as there are people who do it.

I have known several male submissives who take on the role of butler, valet or major domo in a household because they want to serve, not because there is any kind of sexual relationship involved.

FetLife.com is the best place to look to talk to others with similar interests, or just those open-minded about exploring. Join some of the discussion groups, make some online friends, but don't go in thinking you will immediately find what you're looking for. Make friends and connections first. Read up on the facts of BDSM. Learn how to describe what it is you are looking for clearly, using the right terminology.

For example, you might not want to use the "bear" example. While I understand what you mean completely, in the gay community a "bear" generally refers to hairy men and those who love them.

In my own corner of the kinky world, just about every fem domme I know would love to have submissive who is more interested in serving and pleasing than getting their sexual needs met. Real dommes (those who don't do it for the money) are not at all like what you see online in porn and webcam sex services. Just be patient and learn more about all aspects of BDSM so that you can clearly communicate what you want and what you don't want. I think you'll find a compatible mistress – or master – out there.

KATE KINSEY

33 CAN I BUY A SLAVE FROM A CURRENT OWNER?

Kate:

I was recently introduced to the BDSM world by someone I met online. I have been reading and trying to educate myself. I came across your website and I found it very informative. I am hoping you can set me straight as to whether something is normal in the BDSM world or not.

This woman approached me on an adult website, said she was a submissive sex slave and was looking for an older man in hopes of forming a dom/daddy relationship. After quite a few emails we eventually exchanged phone numbers. I was expecting to talk on the phone and eventually meet her in person.

She belongs to a mistress and according to her mistress's rules, she was only allowed to text. I tried calling the phone number. The account was set up for texting only. We texted for weeks and really got to know each other. I asked upfront if there was a fee; I was told no. Now she wants to come and live here, and wants me to pay a fee of $1,500.00 to her mistress and her mistress will transfer ownership along with documents that I am expected to sign.

I have explained to her that slavery is illegal and I would not pay this fee. I offered to come to where she is located in the US (Bethany, Ok a suburb of Oklahoma City). I was told that she was not allowed to visit with me.

We did exchange photos. Now, she says she has to have an additional $1,200.00 paid for tools. I refused to pay this as well.

The latest is $350.00 for body treatments and facials before she can come to me. We negotiated that I would pay half of the fee $750.00 and half upon her arrival. Her mistress was to pay for the plane ticket. I am to send half the fee soon.

I have held back, because for a time our conversations all seem so real and normal, and other times my gut says I am being scammed.

So in the BDSM world is this proper protocol? Can fees to be paid for a submissive sex slave and ownerships transferred? Supposedly her mistress went to West Africa recently and acquired more slaves to train and sell in the US. She told me she went through three years of training.

In your website, if I am correct, you mention ownership, but are fees actually exchanged?

I know nothing about the BDSM world except from what I have learned from going online and reading since I have meet this woman. In fact it was her suggestion that I Google and do research. What I have read in your website makes the most sense. I am far from qualified for to be a dominant, and if I would pursue this with her or some other *submissive, I would be the one who would have to be trained so as to not injure someone. Your comments, please?*

— Jeffrey

Jeffrey:

I'm glad you wrote me. What you are describing is not common practice — except for con artists, that is.

You are definitely being scammed. Do not send this person any money, or give him/her/it any personal information that could be used for identity theft.

As you pointed out, real slavery is illegal. If this "mistress" is indeed finding young women and selling them for profit, that's trafficking. Trafficking is a serious problem today, and many young women and children are actually bought and sold all the time, but it has nothing to do with BDSM. There has been a recent rash of ISIS soldiers on Facebook advertising captured women for sale as sex slaves. Luckily Facebook and other online sites are working hard to shut down this kind of "advertising" as soon as it rears its ugly head, but it still exists.

You may find some people in the kinky community playing with those kinds of fantasies, but we do not support or condone actual slavery in any way, shape or form. You cannot really buy anyone.

It is far more likely that this is someone who scams people like this all day long. I can guarantee you that no one is spending three years on training anybody they intend to "sell" either in fantasy or reality.

When I talk about ownership, I'm talking about the mental mind-set of a fantasy of dominance/submission that involves two or more consenting, informed adults who have negotiated and agreed upon just what that "ownership" relationship means. "Ownership" and "slave" in the BDSM context are just words that are more about the kind of relationship we are striving for, rather than a reality than can actually be achieved.

Please do NOT send anyone money. There are many scammers out there on dating sites of all kinds, and they can be quite convincing. Never, ever, give money to anyone you meet online.

34 WHY CAN'T I SUBMIT?

Hello Kate:

I've been having some issues. My partner and I are both switches.
Though honestly I'm more dominate than anything and it's my natural
disposition.

He wanted to try being dominant in the next scene we tried (one of
the first ones we've done), which I'm completely ok with, other then the
fact that subbing for me is really difficult. It really pisses me off because I
want to do this but for some reason it makes me so frustrated and angry
that I'm being controlled by someone.

Please any tips that you have would be lovely. Thank you!
—sammi

Sammi:

One of two things is happening here. One possibility is that you
are not a switch, you're a dominant. *Only* a dominant. Think
about the situation, and how you feel. **Wanting** to submit is not

the same as **needing** to submit. You can bottom to someone, but submissives really need and want to submit. It doesn't make them feel frustrated and angry, but excited and fulfilled.

The second possibility is that you might possibly be submissive to someone other than your current partner. I believe we all exist on a sliding scale. I am submissive, but not to just anybody. There are dominants that I know personally that I could never submit to, because (imho) I'm more dominant than they are. That's just how the personality works for me. Perhaps you know deep down that he isn't dominant enough to inspire your submission.

There is a third option, I guess. You could be submissive with your current partner, but you simply don't trust him enough at this point to surrender your control to him.

Talk to your partner about how you feel. You absolutely cannot do something like this without being honest about what is going on in your head. It's not fair to either of you.

You might try a very mild and short scene, while talking about what is going on and what you are feeling at every step. Is there something he could say or do that would help you relax into it? Or does the entire situation just not work?

You don't have to be a submissive to enjoy elements of BDSM. You could be a bottom, who enjoys some of the activities like bondage or flogging without ever surrendering your power to anyone else. Read up on the difference between bottoming and submitting, and see if anything there speaks to you that might clarify your feelings.

If it becomes an issue that your partner still wants to take a dominant role, but you don't want to submit to him, perhaps you could find another submissive that you could play with together, with both of you in a dominant role.

But whatever you do, don't fake it. Talk to your partner.

35 WHY ISN'T HE ANSWERING MY TEXTS?

Dear Kate:

I'm very new to the Dom/slave relationship. I'm a virgin to it actually but have unknowingly dabbled in it for years. I'm worried that my Sir hasn't contacted me in 24 hours but I know he's reading my texts. What do I do??? I'm so lost. Do I ask him for a reason or do I just tell him I'm moving on? Please help me!!!!

— Bonnie

Dear Bonnie:

It depends. How much time have you invested in this relationship? Is it a negotiated actual relationship, or just someone you've played with casually?

Not knowing what his obligation is to you, or your's to him, it's hard for me to give you advice. If he has told you he is committed to you and this relationship as your master, then you have every right to ask him what is going on. Though you should do it in a respectful manner. "Master, all you all right? Have I displeased you in some way?"

I'm hoping that your texts have not been whiny, demanding or angry. Dominants don't respond well to any of that.

If he hasn't told you this is a committed relationship, and this is a more casual hookup of little duration, and he's not responded, then it sounds like he's ghosting you. Don't waste another text or thought on him. You didn't just have sex with him for the first time, did you? Because if he's been very attentive until now, and that is the case, then move on.

On the other hand, 24 hours isn't a lifetime. It is entirely possible that he's got something going on that is legitimately taking up his time. Nothing is worse than getting all hysterical and then finding out that he lost his phone, his professional life has exploded, or his mom was suddenly hospitalized. Consider just hanging on for a day or two, and if he still hasn't contacted you, then move on.

Are you sure he's not married or in another relationship? Unfortunately, that often explains dominants who drop off the radar for unexpected periods of time.

36 WHAT DO I WEAR TO A HIGH PROTOCOL DINNER?

Good morning, Kate:

As part of a larger BDSM convention, we will be attending a private dinner with 15 couples. The dominants are expected to be dressed formally. The subs are to be dressed as it pleases their dominants. My Sir keeps kidding about having me wearing superwoman yellow spandex (talk about magnifying all the things I work so diligently to minimize), so he can ogle my ass as I serve him. I'd rather lick the souls of his boots than wear yellow spandex, but I'll do as he pleases, of course.

Anyhow, I've read that during these dinners, some wear revealing clothing, others suggest being more demure and having all the emphasis on the dominants. Nudity is explicitly forbidden from this venue as are sexual activities during dinner.

We want to fit in but it's hard to know which way to go without knowing this particular specific group of folks.

I was thinking of suggesting a black Chinese periwing dress. Do you think this is a good idea, or should I aim for something sexier or more somber and modest?

Your wisdom is appreciated.

Kindest Regards,

—Renee

Renee:

I am hoping he's not serious about the yellow spandex, but only engaging in some mind-fucking to tease you. Aside from making you uncomfortable, my own humble opinion is that if this is your first time —or close to it — socializing with this group, standing out in something so gaudy might be considered a little odd, as if he has a fetish for Big Bird.

I think the Chinese dress sounds lovely. Discuss this with him, explaining that you want to please him but need to be prepared with the right outfit to reflect well on him. Suggest perhaps that the Chinese dress you have in mind makes you feel submissive and attractive, in keeping with a traditional Chinese female role. Point out that if he'd like to help you pick out something else, you need to get started.

If he is serious about spandex, beg him to consider black or red. Seriously. Beg.

How sexy should you go? That's up to him, but you're allowed to mention what level of sexy would make you feel comfortable. My own Sir has told me before that while he can tell me to wear a certain outfit, it's not at all sexy if it's going to make me squirm, tug and itch all night. He'd rather I be well within my own comfort range.

On the other hand, these are just people. Screw 'em if they don't like what you're wearing.

Have fun! That's the important part.

37 HOW DO I KEEP FROM BECOMING TOO DEPENDENT ON MY DOMINANT?

Ms. Kinsey:

I am a recently self-identified submissive male who is really struggling with all the physiological aspects. Your article on sub-frenzy helped me appreciate the potential problems and pitfalls of forgetting to use good judgment when choosing a partner.

In my case, I am going to see a reputable, even renowned, pro-domme, so I am not worried about being with someone who doesn't know what they are doing.

The problem is that I am experiencing physiological sensations that I have never experienced before, even when I was dating in high school! I have constant butterflies, my arms and core just go limp, and I make these involuntary high-pitched noises when I look at pictures of my Goddess.

I am concerned that emotionally I am in over my head and that I will struggle to exist without my Goddess once she is done with me Thursday. This is ironic because in my prior career I was a licensed mental health counselor for 16 years.

What is happening to me? How can I avoid ending up needing my Goddess' love to function in my day-to-day life?

I would appreciate any guidance you can offer.

— Martin

Martin:

If you have a background in mental health, then you understand what it means to be a competent, fully-functioning adult with feet firmly on the ground of reality. If you had 16 years of a career under your belt, then obviously, you are old enough to have reasonably good judgment. So, given all that, if you have no history of going overboard or becoming co-dependent on another person to the point it becomes a damaging influence in your life, then I think you're going to be okay in the long run with D/s relationship.

But I'm sorry, my friend, there is no way to avoid the risk of losing your heart and getting it broken. That's true in any relationship that offers any chance of true joy and growth.

If the domme that you are seeing is good at what she does and truly professional, then hopefully she can help you maintain some kind of balance. Keep in mind that the relationship will be intense in the beginning, but you will gain some perspective as the relationship goes on.

Do you have references on this person from people you actually know? Don't rely solely on what she or her website says about her. There are many who are wonderful people, and they provide an invaluable service in helping many meet their most intimate needs. But there are also those in it purely for financial gain with little care for you as an individual.

Have you made any connections in the BDSM community, either online or real life? A supportive group of friends is one of the best ways to help you keep your balance. Having someone to talk things over with can help a lot, especially when it is someone you can trust to keep an eye out for any erratic or worrisome behavior from you.

Be patient, continue to study, and just go slow.

38 ARE THERE COUNSELORS FOR KINKY FOLK?

Kate:

My husband and I broke up earlier this year and I literally found myself again. :) He begged to come back and shared that he had a need for kink and wanted to serve. (Apparently, he liked the life we were leading without him more than where he was heading.)

As there are rules in all relationships, the rules of his return were negotiated and absolute. These rules were negotiated as a family before he moved back. (Obviously, the kinky side of things was not an open subject.) Unfortunately, these lines are once again becoming blurred and we have a power struggle starting once more, both inside and outside the bedroom.

Are there any resources available (i.e. marriage/relationship counselors) that work with these types of complicated, and more common than one would think, relationships?

Thanks!

— *Maisie*

Maisie:

Yes, there are kink friendly counselors, though how accessible they are depends on where you are located. The National Coalition for Sexual Freedom has a section on their website for kink-aware professionals of all kinds, including counselors and therapists. I've included the link below.

https://ncsfreedom.org/resources/kink-aware-professionals-directory/kap-directory-homepage

These are professionals who have varying levels of experience but are friendly to kinksters, and have joined this listing precisely because they want to help kinky folks. If there is no one in your city or town, call someone nearest to you and ask if they can recommend anyone.

I hope this helps. Good luck.

39 DO US BOTH A FAVOR

After reading this book, you may be considering asking your own question via my website. Do us both a favor, okay? Make sure your question isn't one of the following:

1. How do I get started as a submissive/in BDSM?

Please see *How to be a Healthy and Happy Submissive* by yours truly. I've already put everything I know into that book about how to get started. There's nothing left in that cupboard. Honest.

2. How do I find a dominant?

Please see Question 1 above.

3. Can you give me some advice?

Probably. But you'll need to be more specific. Advice about what, exactly? Wine selection? Movie choices?

4. I am looking for someone to mentor me.

I wish you luck. As much as I might like to help, I simply don't have the time or resources to personally mentor someone online.

Remember: a mentor doesn't want to have sex with you. Or maybe they want to, but they don't try to.

5. I am a secondary submissive, but I know he's going to leave his primary—

Uh, no. He isn't. How do I know this? Because they never do. And if he does, you shouldn't want him, because he's just going to leave *you* for the next one and you're going to be miserable waiting for that shoe to drop.

40 REMEMBERING SHIRLEY BECK

If you have already read *How to be a Healthy and Happy Submissive*, then you know about Shirley Beck and what happened to her. If you haven't, let me give you the general story, because I have some additional information to add.

In June of 2014, a woman named Shirley Beck died in Clarksville, TN. The story immediately grabbed our attention locally because it involved BDSM, but when the details started coming out online and in the paper, it made me sick – sick in my heart, sick in my soul – in a way I don't think anything else ever has. For weeks, I couldn't stop thinking about the last four hours of Shirley Beck's life.

Four hours. That's how long it took her roommates to beat her to death.

Shirley Beck, age 39, was a "house slave" to six roommates, including a woman named Cynthia Skipper that Shirley called "mistress."

On June 26, three of the roommates beat Shirley to death while Cynthia Skipper watched and egged them on.

It started because one of the men living in the house, Alphonso Richardson, saw a residue on some cups that he believed was the boric acid they used for killing cockroaches. He woke up everyone in the house, shouting that Shirley was trying to kill him and his girlfriend, and that she needed to be punished.

Beck was hung up, gagged, choked and beaten continuously for four hours. Martial art kicks, a bamboo rod, oxygen tubing and a metal pole were among the weapons used on her.

The story only gets worse.

The beating started in the bedroom, but when Beck "leaned" into the television, they moved her to the kitchen because they were worried about the safety of the electronics.

Beck passed out three times, but they thought she was "faking it."

They took photos of Beck, her body battered and broken, hanging from the ceiling.

This haunts me because a human being died, but it hurts even more because I know that yearning to serve, to be willing to accept pain and even cruelty for the sake of another's pleasure.

I'm not really much of a masochist. I suffer in order to please my master, and I know what it is to just keep breathing, trying to endure. To simply hang on through the next blow, and the next, in the knowledge that it will finally end and I will be rewarded with a kiss, a smile, a tender embrace from the master who has never, in all these years, violated my trust.

What keeps tearing at my heart is that Shirley Beck hung there for four hours, just trying to endure. Four hours. There would be no tender caresses or aftercare when it was done. No one would tend her injuries with smiles. No one would say, "I am proud of you."

She didn't have just bruises; she had 13 fractured ribs, a lacerated liver, and a fractured sternum. They said she did not use her safeword – which was her son's name – but they couldn't really be sure because she had a sock stuffed in her mouth the entire time.

She gave her trust to the wrong people. Maybe she went looking for BDSM for all the wrong reasons. But that doesn't make what happened her to any less tragic. She still wanted to be a good submissive. She wanted to offer her body, heart and mind up in service to someone that valued her.

For Shirley Beck, the suffering just went on and on. She died in pain and completely alone.

When tragedy hits in our kinky community, it is almost always an accident born from ignorance, negligence or just blatant stupidity. People just didn't think. Or maybe they were being as careful as they could be, and fate just fucked them over with some accident no one could have seen coming. It happens, and many of us hope that someone will not be crucified just because the justice system and the vanilla world don't understand what it is we do.

But this was not negligence or ignorance; this was just brutality. This case is the very worst of what the world thinks we are, and what they believe we do. It doesn't matter that these people, while known to some of us, were not really a part of our community, and that their behaviors have crossed so far beyond the bounds of decency that we would hardly call them human beings, let alone practitioners of sane, rational and consensual BDSM.

But this case was not really about BDSM or kink. It was about criminal inhumanity. Eric Yow, attorney for one of the killers, tried to introduce BDSM as a "mitigating circumstance," but Circuit Court Judge Jill Ayers didn't allow herself to be distracted by sensationalism. She saw the case for what it was.

"Ms. Beck was beaten to death," said the judge, "and that's the bottom line here."

In April of 2016, Shirley Beck's killers were convicted.

Mathew Lee Reynolds was convicted of first degree premeditated murder, first degree murder, and especially aggravated kidnapping; he was sentenced to life in prison.

Cynthia Diane Skipper, the so-called mistress, was convicted on two counts of criminally negligent homicide with the maximum sentence of two years, and especially aggravated kidnapping, for which she received the maximum sentence of 25 years.

That Cynthia Skipper's name in all the papers is linked to the word "mistress" makes me see red. She did not then or now deserve anything even close to that title. She wasn't fit to own a goldfish, let alone a submissive or slave.

Derek M. Vicchitto, Skipper's fiancée, was convicted on two counts of facilitation of second degree murder (maximum 12 years) and especially aggravated kidnapping (maximum 25 years). The judge allowed these sentences to run concurrently after his parents testified that he was legally blind, suffered from cerebral palsy, and had tested at a very low IQ. I suspect that he was another less obvious victim of Skipper's manipulation and probable abuse.

Alphonso Richardson, the man who started it all by screaming that Shirley had tried to poison him, was convicted of first degree premeditated murder, first degree murder, and especially aggravated kidnapping. He received life in prison, followed by an additional 25 years for kidnapping.

Richardson was the one who beat Beck with the metal pole, a fact that prompted Judge Ayers to say that society needed to be protected from him. He was given no possibility of parole or release for at least 51 years. After that life sentence, the 25-year sentence for kidnapping will begin.

Assistant District Attorney Robert Nash asked Richardson if

kicking and punching weren't enough, that he had to go get a pole?

Richardson said yes; he said he was "in a rage."

Richardson since claims that he has found Jesus in prison, and that he "knows in my heart that she (Beck) forgave me."

I can't even find the words.

I pray they all have long, miserable incarcerated lives in which to remember the life they took so brutally. I regret that taxpayer dollars will shelter, feed and clothe these animals when they should be shot like rabid dogs.

Remember Shirley Beck. Be safe. Be kind. Reach out to those on the margins who seem isolated. Speak out when you see abuse. Share your knowledge and experience with those seeking it.

If we don't treat each other with compassion, who will?

ABOUT THE AUTHOR

Kate Kinsey, best-selling author of *How to be a Healthy and Happy Submissive*, has been an author, educator and collared submissive in the kinky world for more than 15 years. She has presented classes and demonstrations both locally and nationally, and has counseled hundreds of kinksters both online and off.

Her novel, *Red*, has gathered praise for combining top-notch suspense with sizzling sex, as well as its honest portrayal of the BDSM community.

Kinsey is a frequent guest on KinkyCast.com, a podcast dedicated to all things kinky. You can listen to her interviews with Gloria Brame, Laura Antoniou, Nina Hartley and Ernest Greene, John Baku and more at www.kinkycast.com.

As always, you can find more Kate Kinsey on Facebook and her website: www.katekinsey.com

Manufactured by Amazon.ca
Acheson, AB